BRONCHOS TO SPURS

SPORTS IN SAN ANTONIO
SINCE 1888

T0126160

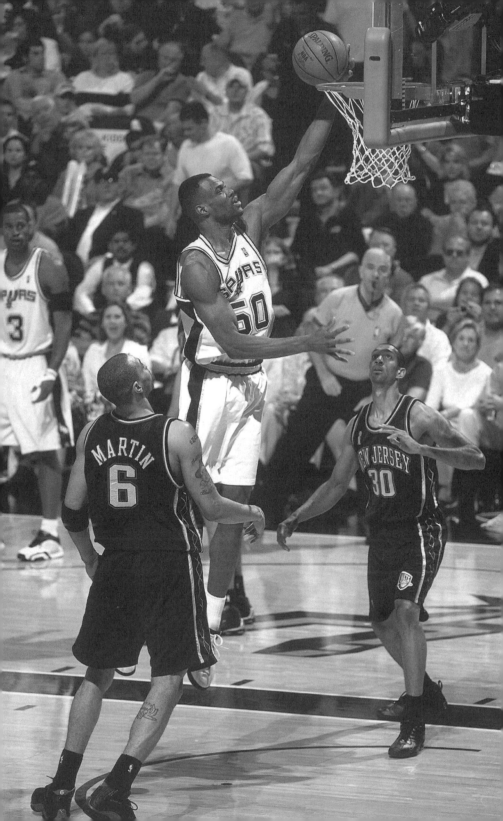

Bronchos to Spurs

Sports in San Antonio
since 1888

Chris Foltz

MAVERICK PUBLISHING COMPANY

MAVERICK PUBLISHING COMPANY
P.O. Box 6355, San Antonio, Texas 78209

Library of Congress Cataloging-in-Publication Data

Foltz, Chris, 1972-
  Bronchos to Spurs : sports in San Antonio since 1888/
  Chris Foltz.
    p. cm.
Includes bibliographical references and index.
  ISBN 1-893271-31-5 (alk. paper)
  1. Sports–Texas–San Antonio–History. 2. Sports–Texas–San Antonio–Statistics. 3. Athletes–Texas–San Antonio–Biography. I. Title.
  GV584.5.S34F65 2003
  797'.09764'351–dc22

                                                    2003021125

5 4 3 2 1

Frontispiece: San Antonio Spurs center David Robinson goes for a layup against the New Jersey Nets during game two of the 2003 NBA finals in San Antonio's SBC Center. The Spurs won the series—and their second NBA championship.
NBAE/GETTY IMAGES

Contents

Preface

With the Spurs coming off their second National Basketball Association championship, the time seems right for a look at how the San Antonio major sports scene arrived at this remarkable point.

From spare time research I'd done on the San Antonio Missions baseball team and the Texas League, I knew that professional baseball had been around in the city since the first team in 1888. It was the Bronchos who brought San Antonio its first sports championship when they won the Texas League title in 1897.

Basketball is a fairly new major team sport in town, having arrived with the Spurs franchise in 1973, so it wasn't hard to follow its trail. There the difficulties began.

San Antonians have long been football fans, but the flurry of the city's minor league teams over the last three or four decades—particularly the Toros—left many vivid memories but no coherent records that could be found. A few scattered programs turned up, but piecing together when the teams came and went and how they performed while they were around took many hours in the sports files and microfilms of the main library, checking out game after game.

Minor league hockey also has a checkered record, though shorter than that of football. Boxing material proved easier to assemble, and reveals a sport with a local history rivaling even the richness of baseball's.

David Robinson, Tim Duncan, George Gervin and other Spurs are destined for San Antonio sports immortality. Others who should already be there are being rediscovered, such as the Black Bronchos' Smokey Joe Williams, who went on from San Antonio to dominate pitching in the Negro leagues and who finally made it, posthumously, to the National Baseball Hall of Fame in 1999.

This book recognizes familiar players as well as brings to light once-celebrated but now often-forgotten San Antonio star players and championship teams.

1. Sports in San Antonio

In today's fast-paced sports world, San Antonio's Spurs are no strangers to the top spot. In 2003 they became National Basketball Association champions for the second time in five years.

Behind their record is a long San Antonio professional and semiprofessional sports history.

San Antonio's first formally played sports, like those of the rest of the country, are rooted in baseball. The game came to the

city two decades after the Civil War and was an instant hit. San Antonio's semi-pro teams disappeared and reformed with such regularity that it's no wonder their weekend fans found its hard to get behind one ball club for any length of time.

The official start of professional sports in San Antonio came with formation of the Texas Baseball League in 1888. Would the venture succeed and would fans pay to see teams play?

Morris Block bought the San Antonio Warriors and helped stabilize the baseball market.

After several starts and stops, by the turn of the century the San Antonio baseball market was firming up. The man most responsible was Morris Block, who became owner of the San Antonio Warriors of the South Texas League in 1905 and who helped in merging the South Texas and Texas leagues and stabilizing the market. During his nine-year association with the San Antonio team, he built a long-lasting foundation for baseball in San Antonio. His business savvy and love of the game also led to construction of Block Stadium, hailed as one of the best minor league ballparks of the time.

One boost to the sport was the staging of up to a dozen or more exhibition games each spring by touring major league teams. With

Babe Ruth sends a ball over the center fence in San Antonio's League Park for a home run that started the New York Yankees toward a 14-4 win over the San Antonio Indians in March 1930.

the major military presence in the city, during World War I and for several years thereafter visiting major league teams were faced not just by San Antonio's minor league teams but also by teams from Kelly Field and from Fort Sam Houston's Camp Travis and post engineer and cavalry units.

One of baseball's all-time stars, pitcher and sportscaster Jay Hanna "Dizzy" Dean, got his start at Fort Sam Houston when he joined the Army at the age of 16. He played for Fort Sam's post laundry team and then for the 12th Field Artillery. When his three years ended in 1926 he pitched for the San Antonio Public Service team before going on to the St. Louis Cardinals and the Chicago Cubs.

A highlight of baseball in San Antonio was the exhibition game in March 1930 at League Park, off Josephine Street north of downtown, when New York Yankee slugger Babe Ruth hit a home run in the first inning. The Yankees won over the San Antonio Indians 14-4.

With baseball entrenched in San Antonio, another sport came into its own—boxing. World champions had long staged exhibitions in and around San Antonio, but by the 1920s a weekly fight card was a common occurrence. Although many promoters tried to gain a foothold in the fight game, one stood out from the rest—Jack Shelton, a former boxer who turned to promoting after his fighting career ended in the 1910s. In his stable of fighters were some who rose to local boxing fame, including Johnny McCoy, Kid Pancho and Battling Shaw.

Many other professional or, in some cases, semi-professional teams debuted in San Antonio during the 1920s, providing a variety of choices in the world of sports. There were the Alamo-Peck Indians in baseball, the San Antonio Rangers in ice hockey, even a semi-pro soccer team that was a precursor to the San Antonio Pumas. The leagues these teams played in may not have been top quality, but they satisfied fans' appetite for sports entertainment until they were wiped out by the Depression. Attendance fell at the ballpark and at local boxing events from the late 1920s through the early 1930s. It would be a while before the fight game regained a strong hold in San Antonio.

Baseball, however, turned the corner with a number of events that stabilized its life in San Antonio. One was a Texas League Championship in 1933. Even more important was sale of the franchise in 1933 to the St. Louis Browns, the first of the many major league affiliations that nourished a minor league farm system still going strong in San Antonio.

With World War II under way, the San Antonio Missions and the rest of the Texas League stopped play for three years, starting up again for the 1946 season. League attendance was at an all-time high, partly due to a sense of return to normalcy and partly just to baseball being America's pastime.

Soon after he joined the St. Louis Cardinals, in the early 1930s the colorful Dizzy Dean returned to sign autographs for his old unit at San Antonio's Fort Sam Houston, where he began playing baseball after he joined the Army.

These years also saw the heyday of boxing, as new boxers emerged on the San Antonio fight scene. Bobby Dykes, Tony Elizondo and Jackie Blair were among a new breed on display in classic fights at Municipal Auditorium.

In 1947 came construction of a new southside ballpark called Mission Stadium. Attendance at major league exhibitions each spring, however, had been dwindling since 1941, when the St. Louis Browns and Boston Braves moved their training camps to Florida and Arizona.

National Football League exhibitions made their local debut in 1949, when the Los Angeles Rams and New York Bulldogs faced off at Alamo Stadium in front of 17,500 fans. The Harlem Globetrotters began their annual tour of San Antonio in 1950, a major event for the city. Football was already a huge attraction around town, as high school and college fans were rabid for the pigskin in any form. For the first time football exceeded baseball as the dominant local sport.

Soon local teams had another force to contend with—television. The TV set changed the way fans chose to view their favorite sport, affecting attendance across the board. Toward the end of the 1950s local fans had to decide whether to watch major league baseball on television or make the sojourn to Mission Stadium.

As the Missions struggled to attract the fans to the local ballpark, the team went independent from the St. Louis Browns for the 1958 season in hopes that a community-owned franchise would be more successful. It wasn't. Sharing a championship with the Amarillo Gold Sox was a bright spot for the Missions in 1961, but things started to go downhill from there.

Despite being affiliated with the Houston Colt 45's beginning in 1963 and fielding great teams with players like Hall of Fame second baseman Joe Morgan, Colt 45's owners felt they were not given the press in San Antonio they deserved to attract fans. They blamed the local media for the eventual franchise move to Amarillo. Houston owner Roy Hofheinz and his general manager, Paul Richards, closed Mission Stadium for good.

With the link to pro baseball gone, San Antonio sports fans found a substitute in 1967 with the start of the Texas Football League. Right away the San Antonio Toros established themselves as the best minor league football team in the Southwest and, some would argue, in the country. The Toros benefited by having mostly homegrown players. More importantly, they were great year after year, beating almost every opponent and developing a fan base that future minor league football franchises would covet.

Before 1967 ended, an old friend returned, as the Chicago Cubs brought baseball back to the Alamo City after a three-year layoff. The new Texas League team, again named the San Antonio Missions, was established largely through the efforts of Elmer Kosub, Dick Butler and Mrs. V. J. Keefe.

HemisFair '68, San Antonio's world fair, not only brought about great exposure for the city; on its grounds was constructed the Convention Center Arena. This venue could at last attract teams and sporting events of all kinds to the city. The Harlem Globetrotters brought their annual game to the arena and the NBA's Houston

Rockets played regular season and exhibition basketball there, planting another seed in the San Antonio sports garden.

Fans' enthusiasm for these early games finally brought a major sport franchise to San Antonio when, in the spring of 1973, local investors purchased the American Basketball Association's Dallas Chaparrals and moved them to a new home in the arena as the San Antonio Spurs.

While local basketball was on the rise, football teams were struggling to remain afloat. The Toros, once the dominant force in the Southwest, encountered financial struggles in the early 1970s, cut seasons short and canceled road games. The one-year experiment of the World Football League in San Antonio ended after 13 games, when six of the ten WFL teams voted to fold the league.

It is worth noting that there have been many football players turned pro wrestlers in the history of pro football, and that San Antonio football teams have produced at least four of them: Leo Seitz (Toros '69), Bill Lehman aka Seigfried Steinke (Toros '67–'71), John Layfield aka Bradshaw of the WWE (Riders '91), and the most famous of all, Frank Goodish, also known as Bruiser Brody, who played with Toros in 1968.

By the 1970s, times were changing in San Antonio. No longer were minor league teams in baseball and football covered as they once were. No longer did they have the same following from the fans. They were seen as just developmental programs. The real fame, the real glory and the real money across the board was in a major sports team such as the San Antonio Spurs. With the ABA-NBA merger in 1976, fans and media shifted their main attention to the Spurs. There was still football, beginning in 1977 with the American Football Association's San Antonio Charros, but the enthusiastic days of the Toros were gone.

The San Antonio Thunder, the city's entry in the North American Soccer League, lasted but two seasons, 1975 and 1976. They were a mediocre 6-16 and 12-12 when owner Ward Lay moved the team to Hawaii, only later regretting the move. The one local soccer highlight was a March 31, 1976, exhibition game between the Thunder and the New York Cosmos, featuring the celebrated Pele.

Meanwhile, the hapless Missions changed parent clubs and nicknames as they struggled with attendance in an unstable Texas League. Finally, an agreement signed in the winter of 1976 ensured a bright future for San Antonio baseball by making the Los Angeles Dodgers the parent club, an affiliation that would last 24 seasons.

The year 1979 was one to remember for San Antonio sports fans. It ultimately brought more heartache than celebration, but it also yielded thrilling moments we still remember. The Charros were in the thick of things, posting a 10-4 gridiron record and making the playoffs. The Spurs came close to making the NBA finals. The Dodgers lost out in the Texas

Construction of a domed arena for HemisFair '68 at last gave the city a venue for major sports events. Five years later the San Antonio Spurs arrived. The arena's dome was later raised to increase seating capacity before the facility fell victim to convention center expansion. The Spurs went to the new Alamodome before moving on to the SBC Center.

League Championship series. San Antonio's own Mike Ayala, fighting in front of a home crowd, came up short against WBC Featherweight champion Danny Lopez.

Despite all that drama, the next decade saw the San Antonio sports scene struggle. There was no immediate payoff from soccer's attempt to reenter the San Antonio market on March 21, 1981, when the North American Soccer League's Atlanta Chiefs and Dallas Tornado staged an exhibition game at Northside Stadium in front of 5,595 fans.

In football, the Charros ceased operations so the U.S. Football League could award the Gunslingers franchise to the city. For two seasons the inept Gunslingers, led by renegade owner Clinton Manges, faltered in wins, faltered in players' paychecks and became the poster child for poorly run sports franchises.

The Dodgers started the decade in winning fashion but soon were having their own ups and downs. And despite similar promise at the beginning of the decade, Spurs attendance dropped and the franchise seemed to be on its way out of San Antonio. The Gunslingers folded, George Gervin was traded, Johnny Moore contracted Desert Fever and boxer Mike Ayala was a shell of his former self.

But things turned around in the 1990s, as a combination of winning and new teams brought a renewed interest in the local sports scene. Joining the Spurs and Missions as home teams was the semi-pro soccer entry San Antonio Heat, which was succeeded by the San Antonio Generals and finally, from 1993 to 1998, by the San Antonio Pumas. Early in the decade the NFL's Houston Oilers set up training camp in San Antonio, the first time a pro football team had done so. Minor league football returned for a short time in the form of the World League of American Football's San Antonio Riders.

In April 1990 Robert Quiroga became the first San Antonio native to win a world boxing championship by winning the IBF junior bantamweight championship.

By this time, no longer were the Spurs the old offshoots of the renegade ABA; they were earning respect around the league and carrying themselves like no other Spurs team had done before. The team's future had actually been set in 1987, when the Spurs won the NBA draft lottery and selected as their number one pick Naval Academy graduate David Robinson, who became the Spurs' savior and the franchise's greatest player.

Soon the Spurs were traveling by charter plane rather than on commercial flights. There was an increase in the number of Spurs games on national television. And there was a new place to call home, with the move from the HemisFair Arena over to the massive Alamodome, which opened in the spring of 1993 in hopes of luring multisport events and even a National Football League franchise.

The first event in the Alamodome was a U.S. Olympic Festival. The Alamodome could also hold major sporting events such as the Don King mega-fight card in September 1993, and the 1996 NBA All-Star Game. These events proved San Antonio's capability in organizing and presenting the big sports shows which some thought would never come to the Alamo City.

The new San Antonio sports market became one to covet. The Houston Oilers staged training camps here while fighting the built-in fan base of the Dallas Cowboys. On the baseball diamond, in 1994 the Missions moved to a new venue on the Southwest side of town—Nelson Wolff Stadium, an upgrade from St. Mary's University's outdated V. J. Keefe Field, home of the ball club for the previous 26 seasons.

For one season the baseball market was crowded, as San Antonio fans had two teams to follow, the Tejanos and the Missions. But the well-established Missions with their new ballpark won out, and in early 1995 the San Antonio Tejanos packed their bags and moved to Laredo.

But football, the sport that seemed to have a hold on South Texas like no other, couldn't recreate a following like the San Antonio Toros had many years before, as no minor league football team stayed long enough for a sufficient number of local fans to get behind it.

Strangely enough, minor league hockey would stick around and score with local fans once the Central Hockey League's San Antonio Iguanas arrived in 1994. At one point during the 1990s there were even two ice hockey teams San Antonians could call their own—the Dragons and the Iguanas. Who would have thought it—ice hockey in sizzling Texas.

By the end of the 1990s, San Antonio sports success couldn't have been sweeter. In 1997 the San Antonio Missions won the Texas League championship, their first since 1964. The Spurs, winning the NBA draft lottery again in 1997, selected Tim Duncan, ensuring the franchise's success sooner than they thought. Two years later the Spurs won their first NBA title, becoming the first former ABA team to win that crown.

In 2002 the Missions battled back in the playoffs and won another Texas League championship, this one under a new parent club, the Seattle Mariners. The following season was even better as the Missions won both halves of the season, compiling an 88-51 record and in five games defeating the Frisco Rough Riders for the Texas League championship.

To the disappointment of hockey fans, though, their beloved Iguanas' time was up. The team folded, and diehard Iggy fans had to switch allegiance to a new team, the American Hockey League's San Antonio Rampage. Now there was a new state-of-the-art arena to house both the Spurs and the Rampage, plus other sporting events that could not fill the Alamodome: the SBC Center, which debuted in 2002. The Dallas Cowboys held their first training camp in San Antonio in 2002, the first locally since the Houston Oilers' last camp six years before.

Anchored by Tim Duncan and David Robinson, in his last NBA season, in 2003 the Spurs won their second NBA Championship in front of hometown fans by defeating the New Jersey Nets. It had been a long road in San Antonio sports since the first games on the dusty, primitive ball diamonds of the 1880s, but this second championship confirmed the once-shaky belief that professional sports could indeed flourish in San Antonio, and cemented the Alamo City's record as a triumphant professional sports town.

2. Circling the Bases

San Antonio professional baseball dates back to the days when exhibition games were played by major league clubs on barnstorming tours of Texas. The most notable of these was played by the St. Louis Browns, led by legendary manager Charlie Comiskey, in a game at San Pedro Springs in the winter of 1885 on the team's way to the West Coast.

Soon baseball teams were popping up all over, including the San Antonio Sunsets, a semi-pro team composed of railroad men, soldiers and lawyers which included the likes of Charlie "Smokey" Palmer, "Long John" Green and "Judge" Billy Anderson.

With baseball firmly planted in Texas, an enterprising baseball man named John McCloskey, who put on a successful barnstorming tour of his team from Joplin, Missouri, launched the Texas League, the state's first organized league. Included was a team from San Antonio. The original team posted a record of 6-28 before disbanding. A second team, a relocated Austin franchise, compiled a 14-11 record but withdrew from the league in August, as team failures throughout the league seemed to occur on a regular basis.

Pitcher Frank J. Hoffman, who led the Texas League in strikeouts with 231 in 1888, became the first San Antonio player to graduate to the big leagues when he joined the American Association's Kansas City team in late 1888.

Following in the footsteps of the San Antonio Sunsets was a long list of amateur and semi-pro teams, including the San Antonio Browns, Havanas, Crescents and Jokers. While many flourished along the way, the amateur team with the most staying power—1886 to 1891—was the San Antonio Jokers, led by manager Frank Huntress.

In 1891 the Jokers transformed themselves into a semi-pro team captained by former major leaguer Jack Phelan. In 1891 the Jokers were at their peak, defeating every opponent put in front of them and becoming one of the best teams in the state. Phelan went on in the mid 1890s to organize other strong semi-pro teams.

It wasn't until the late 1890s that a winning San Antonio franchise started to take shape. The person who made the difference was first baseman Mike O'Connor. The Marion, Ohio, native first appeared in a San Antonio uniform in 1892 and became manager of the San Antonio Bronchos (then spelled with an unpronounced "h") in 1897.

At 6'5" the imposing O'Connor was a dangerous hitter, in 1896 leading the Texas League in batting (.395) and home runs (18). His tenacious batting proved a key to San Antonio's success in 1897, when the team received the nucleus of the Denison ball club, a Texas League dropout. Among the talented players arriving in San Antonio were Charles Weber, Billie Kohnle, King Bailey, Matt Stanley and Win Clark.

Compiling a record of 68–44 (48–16 home, 20–28 road) the Bronchos won the Texas League championship in 1897 despite some events that tainted a great season. At the end of June the Bronchos were so far ahead that the league decided to split the season. Manager Mike O'Connor sold his star second baseman Win Clark to Louisville of the National League for $1,500, thereby weakening his talented team.

San Antonio was eventually dropped by the league, and Galveston, in sole possession of first place at the time, was declared co-champion along with San Antonio. Though slowed in the second half, the 1897 Bronchos' run was one of the best in San Antonio history.

Three little-known events in these years deserve mention. In 1897 the first night games were played on the local diamond, and they became a regular occurrence in 1930. In 1898 the Cincinnati Reds conducted spring training in San Antonio, marking the first time a major league ball club trained in San Antonio. And right after the turn of the new century came the first San Antonio native to make it to the major leagues when pitcher Jake Volz debuted on September 28, 1901 with the Boston Red Sox.

San Antonio's first championship team, the Bronchos, pose after being declared Texas baseball co-champions with Galveston at the end of the Texas League's 1897 season.

Members are, from left, top, pitcher Red Herbert, pitcher Tom Hayes, first baseman and captain Mike O'Connor, center fielder Kirby Bailey and third baseman Winfield Clark; center, pitcher George Gilpatrick, second baseman Charles Weber and catcher Matt Stanley; and, sitting, left fielder Bill Kohnle, shortstop Louie Knau and right fielder George Keefe.

In front is Joe, the mascot, or batboy. At lower left is the team's "assistant mascot," a racoon named Zip.

Stability in ball clubs and leagues that San Antonio played in finally materialized in 1903, when San Antonio was a member of the South Texas League. Having adopted the name Mustangs, San Antonio, led by owner-manager Wade Moore, also the catcher, was poised to make a run for a championship. The team was comprised of such solid players as first baseman Pat Newnam, leftfielder Eddie Gallagher and superb pitcher William "Lucky" Wright.

The Mustangs finished the year at 69-54 and went on to win the 1903 South Texas League championship by defeating Galveston in the playoffs 7 games to 2, after the series was cut short due to poor attendance and despite swirling allegations of gambling and illegal use of players. The series highlight was San Antonio pitcher Eddie Taylor's no-hitter in game six.

As difficult as it was when it came to equipment and travel in those early days, add this to the list: the ball clubs' rosters did not exceed 12 players and the salaries were not to exceed $1,000 a month for the entire club.

Meanwhile, in 1907 the San Antonio Black Bronchos began making their own history under the ownership of local business-man Charlie Bellinger, who assembled his team and played at Electric Park south of San Pedro Park, when the white Bronchos went on a road trip. In their 1907 series meeting the Black Bronchos' defeat of the Birmingham Giants culminated in a 13–4 record and championship of the South.

The Black Bronchos repeated as champions of the South and added championship of the state when they defeated Dallas Black Giants in 1908. Their record stood at 35-8, and they seemed unstoppable. In 1909 they again found themselves in the state championship series, against the Houston Black Buffs, though the result of that series is unknown.

Throughout the Black Bronchos' existence, their success stemmed from one individual, whose pitching exploits would become legendary for years to come: "Smokey" Joe Williams. Williams soon joined the Negro leagues for a long and prosperous career that later rivaled the great pitcher Satchel Paige. His legendary pitching prowess made him rank in a poll taken in 1952, a year after his death, as the greatest pitcher in the history of black baseball. In 1999 he was enshrined in the Baseball Hall of Fame.

When he began his baseball career with the Black Bronchos the glory years in local black baseball had only started, but Smokey Joe was the foundation on which later San Antonio black teams and players could proudly stand.

With the merger of the South Texas and Texas Leagues in 1907, the San Antonio Bronchos' future looked bright thanks in large part to its enterprising owner, Morris Block, who came on board after purchasing the then–South Texas League's San Antonio Warriors in 1905 for $700. Block came to San Antonio after the great Galveston hurricane and flood of 1900 and opened a cigar store on Alamo Plaza. An ambitious and savvy owner, he made the Bronchos profitable for the first time.

The 1908 season saw the greatest success yet as the Bronchos won 95 games under their legendary manager, George Leidy. He gave up the reigns of manager, but returned to lead his team to the Texas League championship. "Cap," as Leidy was called, could develop young ballplayers like no other and later became a scout for several major league ball clubs, bringing such stars as Eddie Cicotte and Ty Cobb into baseball's mainstream.

Smokey Joe Williams, in a New York Lincoln Giants uniform, started with San Antonio's Black Bronchos and went on to national pitching fame in black baseball.

The 1908 Bronchos squad had great talent, with first baseman Pat Newnam leading the league in home runs with 18, and with right fielder Sam Stovall and third baseman "Tex" Wisterzil, at 17 fresh out of high school. But it was the pitching staff that deserved most of the credit: Fred Winchell who was 20-11; Roy Mitchell; "Buck" Harris; and fireballer Harry Ables, who finished with 15-6 record. It was in August that the Bronchos finally pulled away from their neck-and-neck race with the Dallas Giants for first place and reeled off 17 straight victories to take the pennant.

The season was so successful that proceeds from the campaign were used to build San Antonio's first modern ballpark. Block Stadium, just south of downtown at 1415 South Presa Street, was such a hit in the baseball community that the likes of Connie Mack, John McGraw and Ford Frick praised the new home of the Bronchos and all its glory.

Over the next decade the franchise stayed above .500, but only once were the Bronchos in the hunt for the pennant. First baseman Frank Metz emerged as the team's star in 1912. He eventually led the Texas League in battling (.323) and in home runs in back-to-back seasons—1911 (22) and 1912 (21). To go with Metz, talented Broncho ballplayers included centerfielder Tony Thebo, shortstop Charles Seitz and catcher Charles "Goldie" Betts, who 14 years later gained fame as a player for the semi-pro San Antonio Sunsets in the Southern Pacific League.

The 1912 pennant race included the Houston Buffs, consistent all year long in large part due to a well-balanced attack of base running and pitching, especially by star pitcher George Foster, who led the Texas League in wins. The Buffs took the lead for good on May 20 and never looked back.

San Antonio may have lost the pennant due to a poor season's start, but with a weak outfield, no left-handed pitcher and an already short-handed pitching staff, the numbers were stacked against them. In 1915 Morris Block sold the ball club to Harry Benson and his associates for $15,000, ending the Block-Leidy regime.

Through the World War I years and into the jazz age the San Antonio teams were less than average, with just a few seasons of brilliance. Individual performances were still plentiful, such as those of Emmett Munsell, who had 25 wins in 1915 after losing 27 the year before; leftfielder John Baggan, who played in a record 508 consecutive games between 1915–1918 only to have his streak stopped by joining the Army; versatile catcher Fagan Burch; and leftfielder Everett Booe, whose association with San Antonio lasted seven years.

One player's offensive exploits would resemble the 1920s offensive surge like no other—those of the legendary Ike Boone.

The Alabama native had already showed signs of devastating hitting in other minor leagues, but Boone's fourth professional season with San Antonio was perhaps his greatest. The leftfielder dominated the Texas League circuit in 1923, finishing with a .402 average and driving in 135 runs with 241 hits, not to mention a 35-game hitting streak from June through July.

These feats earned Boone a shot at the big leagues when he was sold to the Boston Red Sox at season's end. The fact that he did not stick around the majors was in large part due to his defensive abilities, which were suspect. In the end Boone did establish the minor league career record for batting average, with .370.

Legendary San Antonio Bears hitter Ike Boone went on to the Boston Red Sox.

On the semi-pro circuit, the one team that became legendary among the San Antonio faithful was the Alamo–Peck Indians. Active from 1922 to 1925, the Indians were the brainchild of George Schwab, an Alamo Furniture Company executive who headed the ball club until he sold his interest to Harold Winters.

On the Indians roster were the likes of Joe Straus, who became successful in the horse-racing world; George Huntress; Jimmy Brought, who later taught Dizzy Dean the ways of pitching; Ike Pendleton, no stranger to San Antonio baseball; future major leaguer Pinky Whitney; Tim Griesenbach; and Tex Wisterzil, who took over the managerial reigns from Ike Pendleton in 1925. Championships were plentiful throughout the Indians' tenure. Their place in San Antonio memory as one of the greatest semi-pro teams ever organized is well deserved.

In the local black minor leagues, the San Antonio Black Aces had a budding superstar on their roster. Shortstop Willie Wells began his career with the Aces in 1923 and went on to play shortstop for many years in the Negro leagues, most notably with the St. Louis Stars. Years later he was inducted into the National Baseball Hall of Fame.

In the decade of the 1920s, the acts of generosity and tribute were on display in San Antonio when two events occurred. After Hall of Fame pitcher Rube Waddell died of tuberculosis in 1914 while convalescing in San Antonio, he was buried at Mission Burial Park with a simple marker practically unnoticed until San Antonio Bears owner Harry Benson started a movement to replace it. In August 1923, local fans, leagues and even men such as Connie Mack and Benson, whose final resting place is but a few feet away from Waddell's, all contributed to erect a magnificent granite monument to one of the more eccentric pitchers in baseball history.

The same gesture was repeated in 1935 for Hall of Fame outfielder Ross Youngs, who died in 1927 of a kidney ailment. The idea was to play an exhibition game with all the proceeds going to a new monument, so on September 15 a game was played at Tech Field between the San Antonio Bombers and the Somerset Grizzlies, both of the Fat and 40 League, with tickets going for 25 cents. Grizzlies Manager Walter Comstock was a schoolmate of Young's while the two attended San Antonio's Main Avenue High School.

Another benefit game was planned later in Shiner, Texas, the birthplace of Ross Youngs. Local baseball players past and present like Harry Ables, Jimmy Brought, "Goldie" Betts, Jim Riley and the legendary Ike Pendleton paid tribute to a baseball hero who will never be forgotten.

The early 1920s was a time for offensive play around the Texas League. San Antonio was no different. It began with Ike Boone in 1923 and carried over to 1925, when second baseman Danny Clark led the league in batting (.399). Along with Clark on the squad were some of the best players San Antonio had ever seen, like short-stop Mike Gonzales, centerfielder "Moke" Meyers, leftfielder Lyman Nason, first baseman "Mule" Washburn and catcher Firmin Warwick.

Unfortunately these Bears teams were playing at a time when the great Fort Worth Panthers and their dynasty dominated year after year, eventually leading the other great ball clubs and players to be easily forgotten.

Some of this play was under the first woman president of a Texas League team. When San Antonio Bears owner Harry Benson died in 1924, he left his wife, Mabel, to run the ball club. Soon after, though, former Bronchos pitcher Harry Ables bought the ball club from Mrs. Benson, for $85,000.

With the start of the 1926 season, Texas League writers were picking the Wichita Falls Spudders as the favorites to win and the San Antonio Bears to finish last. Bears owner Harry Ables thought differently. After all, his old battery mate from his days in the Pacific Coast League, Carl Mitze, was now his manager.

Sure enough, out of nowhere came the San Antonio Bears, with steady shortstop Ray Flaskamper, centerfielder Joe Rabbitt and leftfielder "Ping" Bodie—batting .338 with 105 RBIs—leading the way. Ables' motivation for buying Bodie from Wichita Falls that June was for Bodie to lead the offense the Bears needed for a run at the league championship. Bodie had been a devastating hitter in the Pacific Coast League for many years, and at the time of his arrival from Wichita Falls, where he spent winters as a policeman, he was batting .340.

The Bears split their last regular season series with the front-running Dallas Steers, which included a 12-0 shutout in early September, but they could gain no ground on Dallas. It would be years before San Antonio could climb out of the second division.

During the early 1930s, San Antonio fielded less than stellar teams, causing some to speculate on their future. That all changed when the St. Louis Browns became the first parent club of a San Antonio ball club in 1933 and began a 22-year affiliation. Add to that a new playoff system for the Texas League and the Indians-turned-Missions were poised to take the pennant, led by their manager and longtime major league catcher Hank Severeid.

The 1933 Missions' exceptional ballplayers included leftfielder Larry Bettencourt, centerfielder Pid Purdy, second baseman Ollie Bejma, third baseman Harland Clift, pitcher Abe Miller and pitcher Fabian Kowalik, for a short time the mayor of Falls City, Texas. Their well-balanced attack proved successful as, with 79 wins, they won the Texas League championship by defeating the Galveston Buccaneers in a 4-2 series.

The 1933 season turned out to be the most successful since the Bears were nosed out by the Dallas Steers for the pennant in 1926. The 1933 season saw Tech Field jammed with spectacular crowds. Fans would never forget the playoff performances of pitchers Fabian Kowalik and Hal Wiltse, both 3-0 in the post-season; cen-

San Antonio Missions leftfielder Larry Bettencourt warms up for a game against Galveston at Tech Field in 1934.

terfielder Pid Purdy, who hit .333; rightfielder "Cap" Crossley, who hit .314 with 8 runs scored; and the great leftfielder Larry Bettencourt, who finished with 11 postseason RBIs.

About the same time the Bears' black counterparts were making history as well. Just as the great teams of Smokey Joe Williams and the Black Bronchos did earlier in the century, the San Antonio Black Indians went on a masterful run of winning seasons from 1929 to 1931 behind player-manager Reuben Jones. With fine pitching from Charlie Beverly and the timely hitting of Marlin Carter, the Black Indians put on one of the best seasons in their short history by defeating all opponents in the Texas-Oklahoma-Louisiana League, later known as the Texas Negro League.

After the Black Indians came the San Antonio Black Missions, a team that would become a mainstay around town for many years in the 1930s and 1940s. The one constant throughout the Black Missions' success was Bill Haynes, who began his career as a pitcher for many of the black San Antonio teams of the 1920s and later was installed as manager. He developed local talent from then until 1947, when he moved to Kerrville to manage its area's teams. The mark he left on local black baseball is an important contribution, as was his fostering of the game at a time when blacks were kept out of organized baseball.

Despite the woeful years of the Depression, there were bright times ahead for San Antonio baseball fans. Major league ball clubs were being lured to San Antonio for spring training because of the new Tech Field ballpark, just south of San Pedro Park near the old Electric Park field. Also appearing were many of the all-black teams that barnstormed in San Antonio for years to come. Major credit for this goes to Lorenzo Cobb, a longtime executive in the Negro leagues who relocated to San Antonio and brought their games to town from 1944 to 1953.

Despite winning more games—89—than the year before, the Missions failed in their 1934 bid to repeat when they lost to the Galveston Buccaneers in six games in the Texas League finals, despite the play of star first baseman George "Buck" Stanton, centerfielder Chet Morgan, slugging leftfielder Larry Bettencourt and pitchers Hal Wiltse, Ash Hillin and Earl Caldwell.

It was another four years before the Missions found themselves in the league championship, this time losing a nail-biter in seven games against the Beaumont Exporters. Stars on that team were centerfielder Ed Silber, shortstop Sig Gryska and second baseman

Johnny Berardino, along with right-handed pitchers Bill Trotter, Jack Kramer and Harry Kimberlin.

From 1937 to 1940 the Missions went on quite a run. Led by their venerable manager, Zack Taylor, the Missions made the playoffs every year, only to be ousted before realizing the glory of a Texas League championship.

From heartbreak to the bizarre, if there ever was a moment to recall from the days leading up to World War II it was the night game between San Antonio and Fort Worth on April 26, 1940. When Fort Worth centerfielder Buster Chatham hit a grounder. Seeking a double play, Missions second baseman George Hausmann threw to Missions catcher Benny Huffman to force Fort Worth player Charley Baron as he sprinted home. Home plate umpire Bill Wilson called the runner safe, saying Huffman did not stand on the bag when he caught the ball, thus giving Fort Worth a 2–1 win.

Huffman, furious over the call, got in Wilson's face, as did other Missions players. The panicked Wilson drew a knife, but somehow Missions manager Marty McManus was able to break things up and prevent an even bigger skirmish.

Beginning in the 1940s, among the many San Antonio black semi-pro teams came into existence were Greer's All-Stars, the San Antonio Eagles, San Antonio Indians (managed by Levy Taylor), the San Antonio Bombers and, in 1948, the O'Connell Jewelry Black Sox, later called the Black Sox and managed by Royal Brock. Without a doubt, the most notable of these was the Black Sox, which won the state semi-pro championship in 1950 and changed its name yet again to Rena's Black Sox before settling back on Black Sox in 1956. The team remained active until 1980.

Among the many heroic sacrifices baseball players made during World War II, one story deserves to be told. That of Si Rosenthal is one of the most heartfelt and generous. Rosenthal played rightfield for the San Antonio Bears in 1924–1925. He hit over .300 in each season and played brilliantly, earning a shot at fame with a trip to the major leagues and played for the Boston Red Sox.

Rosenthal enlisted in the Army over-age after his son Irwin "Buddy" Rosenthal, 17, was killed in the First Marine Division's invasion of Gloucester Cape, New Britain, on Christmas Day 1943. During the invasion of Normandy in 1944, his ship struck a mine off the French coast and he ended up a paraplegic. Despite his handicap, in later years Rosenthal devoted efforts to polio drives, aid to the blind, fighting cerebral palsy and countless other charity campaigns. Also active in several veterans organizations, he was praised in his hometown of Boston by Archbishop Richard J. Cushing and by Mayor John F. Collins, who in 1960 declared a Si Rosenthal Day.

Before World War II, San Antonio was such an attractive spring major league training site that legendary New York Giants Manager John McGraw often repeated the San Antonio Chamber of Commerce's statement that "San Antonio is the greatest place in the world to train a baseball club." Climate, drinking water, altitude—all were reasons teams came to the city for spring training.

To encourage the relationship, in 1941 the city built the Boston Braves a ballpark called Pittman-Sullivan Park. But when the team arrived there was very little grass on the field and dressing rooms were inadequate, much to the chagrin of Braves manager Casey Stengel. Then a wet spring caused numerous drainage problems, and the Braves missed significant training time despite attempts to correct them.

After World War II the Braves moved their spring training to Florida, and the Missions' parent club, the St. Louis Browns, followed suit, not wanting to return if no other major league team joined them. Further discouraging the majors was a Texas League ruling requiring visiting clubs to give local teams a bigger cut of gate receipts from demonstration games played in local clubs' stadiums.

The Browns did return, in mid–1949, to hold tryouts for potential ballplayers at Mission Stadium. Neal "Duke" Henderson and John "Sonny Boy" Miles were among the participants.

After being shut down for three years during World War II, the Texas League resumed play and the San Antonio Missions were back in business. The first few years did not prove as promising as those leading up to the war. But that changed in 1950, when the unthinkable happened. The Missions battled all year long to make the playoffs, a goal in doubt until they finally clinched fourth place in the closing month. In the last three weeks of the season they were known as the team that couldn't be beat.

With the likes of first baseman Joe Lutz, leftfielder Frank Saucier, pitchers Lou Sleater and Frank Biscan, and reliever John "Hoot" Gibson, the Missions swept their series with Beaumont 4-0, faced the Tulsa Oilers in the championship round and wrapped up the championship in six games. It was their first league title since 1933, when they also finished fourth in the playoffs.

Star of the deciding game was pitcher John Pavlick. He was 3-0 in the playoffs and ended up 4-1, but his masterful 1-0 three-hit shutout of the Oilers in Tulsa was due to his devastating curveball. Credit also goes to Missions catcher Dan Baich, who called a great game, and of course to their leader, manager Don Heffner, who at one point during the championship stated he was retiring to become a partner in a pottery manufacturing business in El Monte, California. That venture lasted one year before he was back in baseball.

Pitcher John Pavlick's game six shutout won the 1950 title for the Missions.

This was Heffner's third title in four years, but the excitement didn't end there. The team ended up facing the Nashville Vols, champions of the Southern Association, in the Dixie Series. They quickly were down 3-1 in the series, but, as they had before, the Missions fought back, taking the seventh and deciding game 9-5 in Nashville on the pitching performance of Procopio Herrera, who held the Vols hitless the last four innings.

In 1951 the Missions found themselves in the Texas League championship again facing their old rivals, the Houston Buffs. The series ended abruptly when they were swept 4-0.

By this time the San Antonio Black Missions had disappeared, for segregation in baseball was ending. In 1950 the first black San Antonio players—Joe Joshua, John Miles and John Henry Shaw—made their way into organized baseball. On April 12, 1953, catcher Charlie White became the first black ballplayer to appear in a San Antonio Missions uniform, followed two days later by pitcher Harry Wilson.

In a game where brush-backs are a common occurrence and players are scrapping to make it to the big leagues, no other moment in the decade would better exemplify the Oklahoma–Texas rivalry than the game between the Missions and Oklahoma City Indians in August 1954. The drama unfolded in the fourth inning, when Oklahoma player Jim Neufeldt slid safely into second base on a pick-off play. Mission shortstop Witty Quintana fell hard on Neufeldt, and in return Neufeldt slapped Quintana on the back. Neufeldt got up hobbling, and Indians Manager Tommy Tatum walked over.

After checking on Neufeldt, Tatum walked back to the third base line and, as he did, exchanged words with Quintana. Missions manager Don Heffner came out to settle Quintana down. After things calmed, Tatum got into a verbal war with Missions pitcher Ryne Duren who was sitting in the dugout. Then Duren came out and walked into a Tatum punch. Benches cleared and fights broke out on the field. Meanwhile, Missions catcher Don Masterson and Tommy Tatum had started a brawl at home plate.

After 17 minutes police and umpires were able to get things under control. Six players were ejected, as well as manager Don Heffner, but, oddly enough, neither Quintana nor Neufeldt. Manager Tommy Tatum was fined $25 by the league office, as was Heffner. Texas League President John Reeves never came to San Antonio to investigate the incident, relying only on his umpire crew statements. If there was a hero in all this it would have to be Missions centerfielder Jim Pisoni, who took Duren to Santa Rosa Hospital that night for a dislocated jaw. The Missions, by the way, won in dramatic fashion in 11 innings, 8-7, on first baseman Frank Kellert's home run, his 25th of the season.

With the advent of television, the Texas League found itself clamoring for fans' attention. Despite the play of future Hall of Famer Brooks Robinson, who batted .272 with 74 RBIs in 1957, attendance dropped to 93,000. That led the Baltimore Orioles to end the long parent club affiliation that began in 1933, when the Orioles were the St. Louis Browns. The Baltimore organization thought the Texas League itself would not survive.

In 1958 the Missions went independent and touted a community-owned franchise plan proposed and headed by Marvin Milkes, the general manager whose contract with the Orioles had ended December 31 of the previous year. The idea was a stock selling plan, which at first met with excellent response. Even old timers like Pinky Whitney were called in to buy stock to rally the fans.

With no working agreement, Milkes had to hire a manager, arrange for spring training and set up a new office staff, not to mention round up advertising for an all-important ticket drive. The Orioles leased the ballpark to Milkes and let him have ten players to work with. But all was for naught. The 1958 season ended up with financial losses for the ball club and the Missions went broke, losing an estimated $40,000 that year.

The next year the Chicago Cubs agreed to take over as the parent club. They wanted Ray Mueller as manager, but Milkes wanted his man Grady Hatton, who was popular in San Antonio. The one stipulation from the Cubs was that the Missions had to assume Hatton's entire $8,000 salary, which the parent club usually helped pay. To make matters worse, major league exhibition games, which would have brought in $4,000, were not scheduled for San Antonio.

The Missions appeared to be in danger of extinction in 1960 despite a Texas League championship in 1959, thanks to the talents of rightfielder Lee Handley, pitcher Jose Santiago and third baseman Ron Santo (.327, 11, 87), who gave a lift to the Missions when Billy Williams (.318, 10, 79) left on July 3. The team was swept 3-0 in the championship series by the Austin Senators.

Then local beer distributor John Monfrey purchased the team and Mission Stadium for $325,000. The Missions, still affiliated with the Chicago Cubs, began producing considerable talent. In 1961 the team featured first baseman Don Davis, rightfielder Danny Murphy, leftfielder Craig Sorensen and pitchers Ron George and Morris Stevens, who married Arlene Davis, secretary to Missions General Manager Dick King. That year the Missions found themselves in the playoffs, after finishing in third place with a 74-65 record. After knocking off the Tulsa Oilers in five games, they were poised to take on the Austin Senators for the championship.

It was no contest. The Missions swept through Austin in three, winning their first title in eleven years on their way to the Pan-Am Series against the Mexican League champion Veracruz Eagles. After defeating the Eagles 4-2, the future seemed bright for the Missions. That wouldn't be the last title for the local ball club, but its time in San Antonio was running out.

Two years later, John Monfrey sold his interest in the Missions and the stadium to Houston Colt 45's owner Roy Hofheinz. Under the new parent club, the Missions became the Bullets and fielded great teams, beginning in 1963 with centerfielder Ron Davis, third baseman Ed Olivares, pitcher Cliff Davis and second baseman Mike White, who grew up playing on the sandlots of San Antonio as the son of former Missions manager Jo-Jo White. The 1964 San Antonio Bullets were even better, with shortstop Sonny Jackson, pitchers Don Bradey and Darrell Brandon, and first baseman Chuck Harrison, who had played with the Bullets the year before.

Despite losing in the 1963 Texas League finals to the Tulsa Oilers, the 1964 version of the Bullets had it all together. In what has to be one of the greatest teams San Antonio has ever seen, the Bullets went on to win 85 games and dominate every postseason award. All they had to do was win the championship to make the season complete.

With manager Lou Fitzgerald at the helm and future Hall of Famer Joe Morgan (.323, 12, 90) and Chris Zachary leading the way, the Bullets went through the El Paso Sun Kings in four and faced the Tulsa Oilers for all the marbles. Before game two, Texas League President Jim Burris presented trophies to Joe Morgan as MVP and Chris Zachary as Pitcher of the Year, but the Bullets lost the game 6-3. The Bullets would eventually win the championship but leave San Antonio, as owner Roy Hofheinz moved the team to Shreveport and left Mission Stadium empty.

After a three-year layoff, San Antonio was awarded a baseball franchise in the Texas League. Landing the franchise wouldn't have been possible without the combined efforts of St. Mary's University baseball head coach Elmer Kosub, former Texas League president Dick Butler and businessman Nelson Wolff, who later served as mayor of San Antonio and as Bexar County judge. The Chicago Cubs returned as parent club of the reconstituted Missions. It seemed that everything was in place for prosperous times in the Texas League.

But the climate proved hazy for the new Missions team, and the upcoming years proved to be a struggle. In 1972 the Chicago Cubs were replaced as the parent team by the Cleveland Indians, and the team was renamed the San Antonio Brewers. Even though in the first five years the ball club fielded below-.500 teams, that couldn't stop them from leading the Texas League in attendance in 1972, which was a surprise. That credit goes to General Manager John Begzos for somehow attracting fans to watch a woeful team.

In fact, under the tutelage of Begzos and the Brewers, the ball club in 1975 spawned two future San Antonio general managers, Joe Garcia of the Brewers and Mike Boyle of the Thunder.

During the 1973 campaign the Brewers made an exceptional run at the league championship. Although the team played mediocre ball, during the first three months they caught fire, going 42-22 to end the season under manager Tony Pacheco. By winning 82 games, which included a 47-23 home mark, the Brewers earned a playoff berth for the first time since 1964. To show their gratitude, the Brewers gave their manager a new Ford Maverick on what was billed as Tony Pacheco Appreciation Night in September 1973.

With a balanced lineup that included designated hitter Joe Azcue, first baseman Danay Covert, catcher Jeff Newman, second baseman Duane Kuiper and a superb pitching staff that included Jim Kern (11-7), Jim Moyer (11-4) and ace Rick Sawyer (18-5 with 124 strikeouts), it wasn't hard to see why they had success.

But the season ended in controversy. During the deciding game of the league championship, word came down from Cleveland Indians Director of Minor League Operations Bob Quinn that pitcher Bob Grossman was to start the Brewers–Memphis Blues game over scheduled starter and San Antonio native Joel Horlen. At one point at the end of the season, Horlen, who came out of retirement during midseason, reeled off seven straight wins. He won game one of the series and was to pitch game five against the Blues. The Indians thought Grossman was the younger talent and needed to be developed, while the San Antonio contingent wanted hometown boy Horlen for the bigger draw.

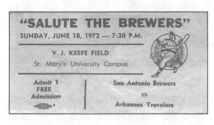

Aggressive promotions helped the Missions–turned–Brewers set a league attendance record in 1972.

In the end the higher-ups won. So did the Memphis Blues, winning the last game 3-2 to take the championship. Manager Tony Pacheco and the rest of the Brewers were left to ponder what if. Brewers General Manager John Begzos resigned over the disagreement and eventually joined the newly formed San Antonio Spurs front office.

Despite great seasons from future stars like pitcher Dennis Eckersley (14-3), league leader in strikeouts with 163 and the league's Right-Handed Pitcher of the Year in 1974, things went from bad to worse. Much to the dismay of Brewers owner Jack Williams, in August 1975 the entire Brewers front office resigned over poor attendance and an all-around dismal season.

So after three tumultuous seasons, the Cleveland Indians pulled the plug on their affiliation, making way for the Texas Rangers to come aboard. But the Texas connection lasted only one season. Not even the magnificent season of Brewers pitcher John Poloni could keep the Rangers in town.

In October 1976 a deal was struck that would stabilize the San Antonio baseball franchise; former major leaguer Wally Moon bought the ball club and signed a working agreement with the Los

Angeles Dodgers. This was the beginning of years of splendid players and numerous playoff trips, though for most of those early years the team would not take the pennant despite talent-laden squads.

The leader for most of the early San Antonio Dodgers years was veteran manager Don "Ducky" LeJohn, who took his team to three straight Texas League finals appearances, from 1979 to 1981. Led by the remarkable play of centerfielder Ron Roenicke, shortstop Gary Weiss and leftfielder Michael Wilson, the 1979 team was the first to make a trip to the championships since the debacle of 1973.

In early 1980 Tom Turner took over as owner of the ball club from Wally Moon and quickly made $200,000 in park improvements to V. J. Keefe Field. But the big story that year was the anchor behind the San Antonio Dodgers, pitcher Fernando Valenzuela, getting called up to the big leagues during the Texas League championship. Valenzuela, with his Carl Hubbell–like screwball, was nothing spectacular early on, but after a mediocre start he went on a roll, winning eight straight games. So, too, did the Dodgers, winning 11 of their last 16 games.

Furthermore, in August Valenzuela was 6-0 with a 0.99 ERA striking out 50 in 45 2/3 innings of work. Backing him up with instant offense throughout the year were leftfielder Dan Holman, first baseman Mike Marshall and centerfielder Tom Beyers, earning the team a shot at the 1980 Texas League championship.

With the Arkansas Travelers leading the championship series two games to none, Valenzuela was to pitch the third game. A day earlier the Los Angeles Dodgers had purchased his contract and said they would allow him to pitch in the series, but they called him up anyway. Arkansas won the game and series, sweeping the Dodgers 3-0. Starting pitcher Brian Holton, who was 15-10 on the year with 139 strikeouts, took the loss in game three.

In 1981, despite posting a 76-57 record and making it to the championship, the Dodgers were swept once again, this time by the Jackson Mets, in three games. The quick exit did not diminish the excellent play of such players as first baseman Greg Brock, third baseman Leo Hernandez, second baseman Steve Sax, leftfielder Dale Holman, rightfielder Mark Bradley and pitchers Tom Niedenfuer and Rich Rodas.

In this same time of great play and renewed interest there were also memorable promotions. On the night of May 27, 1981, the *San Antonio Light* sponsored a contest called Manager for the Night at a San Antonio Dodgers ballgame. It was a very serious event, as Dodgers Vice-President Fred Turner signed eventual winner Christina Stemp, first female manager in San Antonio minor league baseball history, to a one-day $100 contract. The Dodgers were victorious that night, winning 5-1 over the Arkansas Travelers.

Despite having gone to the finals for three straight years, though coming up empty each time, attempts in San Antonio's upcoming years proved futile, as the team reached .500 but once from 1982 to 1987. The one bright spot in all the mediocrity was pitcher Sid Fernandez. In 1983 Fernandez won the Texas League triple crown, with 13 wins, 209 strikeouts and a 2.82 earned run average, no doubt the league's most impressive pitching performance in recent times.

In 1987 the San Antonio franchise went through some significant changes. First, new owner Dave Elmore brought with him a renewed interest in the team as well as a varied sports business background. Plus the ball club returned to its root identity by changing its name from the Dodgers back to the Missions.

By 1990 it was just like old times. The Missions found themselves in the Texas League championship on the strength of rising stars like first baseman Eric Karros, pitchers Mike James and Dan Opperman and eventual Texas League Player of the Year Henry Rodriguez. Although they lost in six games to the Shreveport Captains, many future major league Dodger stars came through San Antonio, most notably catcher Mike Piazza, though his 1992 stay was brief.

At this time days at the antiquated V. J . Keefe Field at St. Mary's University were coming to an end, and talk of a new ballpark were making the rounds. The realization that San Antonio needed to move up to the new generation of ballparks and economics came to fruition in 1994, when Nelson Wolff Stadium opened its doors

In 1947 the Missions began play in the new Mission Stadium, their home for the next 18 years. At the northeast corner of Mission Road and East Mitchell Street, its towers recalled those of the nearby Spanish Mission Concepcion.

for play. Immediately the new digs were a hit, and the Missions led the league in attendance.

When the newly formed Texas-Louisiana League awarded San Antonio a franchise in 1994—the San Antonio Tejanos, managed by ex-Houston Astro Jose Cruz—could San Antonio hold two minor league teams? Having to compete with the more-established Missions and their new ballpark, the Tejanos drew poorly, leading to their demise in February 1995 and an eventual move to Laredo. Again the sole baseball team in town, the Missions' long championship drought ended in 1997, thanks in large part to a fine pitching staff and a second-half surge that carried over to the playoffs.

Led by capable manager Ron Roenicke, whose game time adjustments and player maneuvers helped the Missions go on to win both halves of the 1997 season, the team finished with a marvelous 84-55 record despite suffering from midseason promotions of their best pitchers to the major league Dodgers. Facing their old rivals the Shreveport Captains for the championship, the Missions looked like they were going to sweep the series as they ran up a three game-to-none series lead.

But Shreveport battled back, forcing game seven. In that game, Missions pitcher Will Brunson's three-hit, 2-0 shutout of Shreve-

When the new Nelson Wolff Stadium, facing US 90 in southwestern San Antonio, welcomed the Missions in 1995, design of its twin towers reflected those of the old Mission Stadium that stood some four miles away.

port on the road clinched the team's first championship since 1964. Although it was Brunson's only victory in the postseason, the hurler showed up at the right time.

The title, however, proved to be the last hurrah for the Los Angeles Dodgers in San Antonio. In 2001 the local team opted not to sign with the Dodgers for another season but hooked up with the up-and-coming Seattle Mariners.

That year new blood was on parade at Wolff Stadium. To celebrate their new association with San Antonio, the Seattle Mariners scheduled an exhibition game between themselves and their new farm team, something the Los Angeles Dodgers had never done in all their years as parent club. Also, a new manager was in place—Dave Brundage, a multisport star in his home state of Oregon, who had toiled in the minors first as a player, then as a pitcher.

The 2001 season saw the team reel off 13 wins in row and make it to the playoffs, only to be ousted by the upstart Round Rock Express three games to two. But the following season would be momentous, with the likes of rightfielder Adrian Meyers (.274, 16 stolen bases), centerfielder Jamal Strong (.278, 46 stolen bases) and pitchers Rett Johnson (10-4) and Allan Simpson (10-5, 7 saves). By having a great second half in 2002, the Missions clinched a playoff berth with the never-say-die attitude of the incredible 1950s team.

After winning their opening playoff series with the Round Rock Express, the Missions faced the Tulsa Oilers for the league championship. The series went seven games before the Missions defeated the Oilers 4-1 in front of a home crowd for their first league championship under Seattle Mariners parentage. The hero of game

seven was pitcher Rafael Soriano, whose career-high 14 strikeouts led the way for the home team. The game was redemption for Soriano, who had been promoted to Seattle earlier in the season but sent back down with tendonitis in his shoulder.

The 2003 season got off to a rocky start when slugger Greg Dobbs was lost two games into the sea-

Triumphant in 2003 after the Missions' second straight league title are, from left, players Jose Lopez, Travis Blackley, Luis Ugueto (with trophy), Clint Nageotte, Justin Lamber and Jim Horner.

son due to injury. Early in April the Missions record stood at 2–7, but the key word is "early." The team proceeded to win 22 of the next 24, including a record 18-game winning streak, to sew up the first half-title.

With Dave Brundage back as manager, the squad was well balanced and comprised of players who could do no wrong, with the likes of first baseman A. J. Zapp, outfielder Mike Curry, shortstop José Lopez, Elpidio Guzman and third baseman Justin Leone, the star of the team, who got his chance due to Greg Dobbs's injury. The pitching staff was just as strong, with closer Jared Hoerman, Clint Nageotte and ace Travis Blackley.

After sewing up the league's second half with an 88-51 record, the Missions emerged as powerful as any Missions squad before them and looked to leave their mark on San Antonio baseball history. The accomplishments were amazing: the best pitching staff in the league, Jared Hoerman's 36 saves, speed on the base pads, the league's best double play combination with second baseman Luis Ugueto and shortstop José Lopez, plus manager Dave Brundage's handling of his pitching staff.

The team would face the Frisco Rough Riders for the league championship, and many observers viewed the Rough Riders' chances as minuscule. In a near rout, the Missions outscored the Rough Riders 32-11, including an impressive road win, to clinch the championship with a score of 10-4.

As they did all year, the Missions' offense erupted, battering Frisco pitcher Mario Ramos for a succession of hits and runs to put away Frisco for good in the fourth inning. The winning pitcher for San Antonio, Bobby Madritsch, in six innings of work won his second victory of the series. Coupled with star third baseman Justin Leone's batting .375 for the series, it was a devastating combination, and the Missions' second consecutive Texas League championship.

3. Between the Goal Posts

For some San Antonio fans, the only sport to follow is pro football. It's safe to say that pro football has become the area's dominant sport, giving even the beloved Spurs a run for their money. The Dallas Cowboys have ruled this territory for years, much to the dismay of the old Houston Oilers. The professional football past is a ride that San Antonio fans are sure to enjoy.

San Antonio's first taste of pro football came in September 1949, when the Los Angeles Rams faced the New York Bulldogs in front of 17,500 rabid fans at Alamo Stadium. Sponsored by the *San Antonio Express*, the exhibition was an annual event for five more years. From then on, the NFL and AFL sporadically entertained the San Antonio patronage with more exhibitions. The climate grew right for a local football team. In 1967 the San Antonio Toros took over.

Owned and operated by Alton Fairchild, the Toros were members of the Texas Football League. They played like a well-oiled machine despite having only two players—Hayseed Stephens and Roger Gill—with professional experience. Veteran head coach Duncan McCauley's rock solid team included Luz Pedraza, Roger Gill and James "Bear" Brown

The Toros ran up a 14-0 record and earned a spot in the championship game against the defending champion, the Tulsa Thunderbirds. Early on in the game the Toros were tough, and at the half they enjoyed a 14-7 lead.

Coming out of halftime they were dominant, as their defense stonewalled the Thunderbirds. Toro defensive back Tom Bedick's interception of Thunderbird quarterback Steve Bridgeforth's pass stopped a crucial Tulsa drive. Toros passing was led by quarterback Luz Pedraza (181 yards, including two touchdown passes) and wide receiver Truman Franks, the Trinity All-American (100 yards on eight catches). The Toros gained their first title in their initial year of operation.

Exhibition games were scheduled at the season's end to cash in on the first-year triumphs, but several were cancelled after many Toros players protested that financial rewards were not being met by owner Fairchild.

After several businessmen, including Philip Beurlot, bought into the Toros in 1968, the real news came on the field, when during the season head coach Duncan McCauley resigned to fill the general manager's vacancy with the El Paso football team.

Despite having a 4-0 record, McCauley left a team that didn't miss a beat. The Toros went on to post an 11-1 record and once again found themselves in the championship game, facing the Texarkana Titans. In what turned out to be a wild seesaw battle, the defining moment came down to a stance. Late in the fourth quarter, after a Toros punt was blocked, the Titans regained possession on the Toros' 24-yard line. Texarkana started a drive toward the end zone and soon threatened inside the San Antonio five-yard line with 1:45 left in the ballgame.

With the likes of Ken Hudson, Marc Allen and Bill Lehman forming their formidable line, the Toros held the Titans in check, enabling the Toros to run out the clock and win the TFL championship 21-16. Toros stars were quarterback Luz Pedraza, who passed for 201 yards with two touchdowns, and Rey Farias, who rushed for 38 yards.

Ownership of the Toros changed hands in 1969 as Henry Hight, a local automotive parts businessman, took over the team. The one blemish in their stunning run of championships was the 1969 Continental Football League championship game, when they lost dramatically to the Indianapolis Capitols.

In a game the Toros never led, after a Toro onside kick proved successful they came back from a 10-point deficit to tie the game at 38, on a Jerry Mortiz 38-yard field goal with two seconds left in regulation. However, in overtime Mortiz's 25-yard field goal was wide right with 6:10 on the clock. Indianapolis quarterback Johnny Walton, who would later guide the San Antonio Wings, propelled his team to the title with the help of John Nice, who rushed in for 13 yards with 9 seconds left for the win.

The Toros' success was due in large part to those whose consistent and solid play was never short of great, men such as Bill Grindle, Sal Olivas, Truman Franks, A. C. Lex and R. A. Johnson.

George Pasterchick coached the Toros to four league championships.

The true genius of the Toros' winning machine was their head coach, George Pasterchick, whose passion for football was dwarfed only his integrity and an indomitable spirit. The majority of his life was devoted to football. He played for Trinity University in the 1950s and later was a scout for various NFL and AFL teams.

Pasterchick's introduction to the Toros was as an assistant beginning in 1967. In 1970 he took over a team that already was successful and was able to maintain the momentum. By the time he was done he had guided the Toros to four league championships. In 1971 he became head coach at San Antonio's St. Gerard High School.

In 1970 a new rival emerged for San Antonio football fan: the San Antonio Eagles, members of the United Independent Football League, led by the team's organizer, head coach and quarterback Jerry Wilton. As the Toros had before them, the Eagles proved successful early on, winning championships in 1972 and 1973.

During these years the talent on the team was a who's who of local football talent, with Bobby Roberts, Mano Sommers, Bill Arnold, Clarence Eli and Floyd and Norris Boone. Although the Eagles were comprised mostly of homegrown talent, the Eagles roster was sometimes filled with former Toros.

In the fall of 1970, the 8-2 Toros seemed unstoppable as they faced the Fort Worth Braves for the Texas Football League championship. San Antonio had raced to an early 21–3 lead by the time the second quarter was over. But Fort Worth came back, scoring seven in the third and fourth quarters. That's when the defense of Toro Pat McGill came up big. With Braves quarterback J. D. McMahon throwing inside San Antonio's end zone with 36 seconds left, McGill was able to deflect the football into the hands of neighboring Alfredo Avila, stopping a Fort Worth 62-yard drive and preserving a win for San Antonio.

In a shortened 1971 season, the Toros still found ways to keep winning. In the championship game San Antonio was dominated early on by the Texarkana Titans. But in the second half San Antonio roared back. It was Alfredo Avila again who came to the rescue, with an interception of quarterback Tom Boutwell's pass to spark the Toros with less than five minutes to go in the game. San Antonio was down 19-13 but, led by quarterback Sal Olivas, the Toros drove 66 yards, capped by a Curly Watters rushing touchdown for a fourth Toros league championship in five years.

Among the top Toros highlights came on July 21, 1973 in a game that pitted the 4-0 Oklahoma City Wranglers against the 3-0 Toros. The talk was that if one team could snap the Toros' 15-game winning streak, it was the Wranglers.

For three quarters Oklahoma City dominated the Toros, building a 17-0 lead. What happened in the 4th quarter, with 3:28 left in the game, can be called, simply, unbelievable.

First came a 54-yard drive capped off by a Royce Johnson touchdown that finally put the Toros on the scoreboard. Following a failed San Antonio onside kick, the Toros recovered a fumble by Wrangler Joe Poslick to set up another San Antonio drive, this time resulting in a touchdown pass from quarterback Luz Pedraza to split end Don Burrell. The score became 17-12, with 1:16 on the clock.

Again the Toros went for an onside kick, this time in favor of San Antonio as they recovered on Oklahoma City's 47-yard line. The next Toros drive was highlighted by Luz Pedraza's pass to Roger Gill, who stepped in for the score to put the Toros ahead 18-17, with 19 seconds left in the game. Oklahoma City, with the ball, looked to put an end to the Toros' run. Suddenly Toro left end Bill Grindle sacked Wrangler quarterback Mike Jones, forcing a fumble picked up by Toro Clarence Miles, whose touchdown score put the Toros on the scoreboard once again, with the team eventually winning 26-17.

But overall the Toros were starting to slip. Despite making it to the championship round against the Oklahoma City Wranglers in 1973, the days of the well-oiled football machine were diminishing. In that championship final the Wranglers never trailed. Early in the fourth quarter the Wranglers faked a field goal attempt, enabling them to score and hold on for the win, effectively ending the Toros dynasty.

In the fall of 1973 Toros owner Henry Hight was involved in negotiations to bring the World Football League to San Antonio. But things turned ugly when Hight accused the WFL of tampering with his players and threatened to sue the league for $5 million. In the end the city didn't get the franchise and had to wait until 1975 to see the WFL in action.

Toros quarterback Luz Pedraza was the Southwestern Football League's MVP in 1972.

One memorable 1974 game was the July 20 exhibition between the Toros and the Houston Oilers. The Oilers, comprised mostly of rookies and free agents, won 13-7 in front of 14,209 faithful at Alamo Stadium. The Toros' lone score came with 2:15 remaining when quarterback Luz Pedraza threw a pass to David Yaege. Incidentally, the halftime score was 0-0, and Houston scored all its points in the third.

On the other end of the football spectrum, that same year the San Antonio Eagles made history by signing a female player who actually played in a game.

In 1975 San Antonio welcomed another football franchise to town, the San Antonio Wings. The story began when Harry Lander and Roger Gill met with businessman Norm Bevan in hopes of changing San Antonio's economy and image. Their solution was to relocate the World Football League's Florida Blazers franchise to San Antonio.

The process was not without hurdles. Problems started with an agreement between Toros owner Henry Hight and Wings principal stockholder Norm Bevan which had the Wings paying in excess of $150,000 plus Wings stock in exchange for the Toros team. Weeks later both men accused each other of breaching the contract. Hight went on to say that he never wanted stock but $250,000 cash, while Bevan offered only $20,000.

Hight filed a suit against the WFL for $3 million in damages, claiming breach of contract and that the Wings and WFL monopolized the pro football scene in San Antonio. To make matters worse for Hight, he was losing Toros players and coaches to the Wings, including head coach George Pasterchick.

Hight declared that he would field a team and not fold. In March 1975, however, Hight joined forces with Bevan and sold his interest in the Toros. The Wings went on to attract well at Alamo Stadium, where all their wins came. On the road they were a miserable 0-6, despite being the first team to qualify for the playoffs. But by October the league folded when six of the league's ten teams voted to shut down, San Antonio being one of the holdouts.

The next year Hight tried to bring back the Toros under George Pasterchick in the new Mid-America League, but the team lasted only two games.

In the midst of all this came a flurry of short-lived teams, most formed just so there would be opponents with whom to fill a schedule. Quickly coming and going were the San Antonio Steers, San Antonio Apaches, Texas Thunderbirds and San Antonio Bears, later known as the San Antonio Longhorns.

The San Antonio Eagles were still playing, comprised mostly of former Toros players such as Luz Pedraza, leader of the championship Toro teams a few years before. In 1977 the Eagles packed their bags and moved to Kerrville to become the Kerr County Eagles in 1977; they lasted there only one year before vanishing from the scene, leaving behind memories of such worthy players as the All-American Matt Watell, Clarence Eli and Jerry Wilton.

To fill the void, in 1977 American Football Association President Harry Lander started the San Antonio Charros. Lander was not only owner but head coach, and led his team to the AFA championship with an 8-0 record. The next year former Toro Roger Gill became the owner and former Toros head coach George Pasterchick took the same post with the Charros. Over the next four years the Charros were 28-18, and were always in the playoffs. In 1982 the Charros changed their name to the Bulls to help the team's image in time for their newly signed TV package.

At the beginning of that season the ownership changed hands, as B. J. "Red" McCombs, a Charros investor since 1979, and Tom Turner terminated their association with the Bulls, opening the door for millionaire rancher Clinton Manges and local attorney Pat Maloney to purchase majority ownership. Manges hoped this partnership would bring an NFL team to San Antonio.

During the final game of the 1982 season, with United States Football League President Dave Dixon in attendance, the Bulls launched a promotion called "We Want Pro Football" to start the drive for a better brand of professional football. So it came as no surprise that on July 11, 1983, the USFL awarded a franchise to San Antonio.

The following February the San Antonio Gunslingers made their debut, led by owner Manges, General Manager Roger Gill and Head Coach Gil Steinke. The season looked bright, but the team had no offensive attack and was anemic at best. It failed to make the playoffs.

Their next season was not much better. Head Coach Steinke was made director of football operations while Jim Bates, former Gunslingers defensive coordinator, was named head coach. Things became more troubling when the stadium lights went out during a home game with the Houston Gamblers as a nationally televised ESPN audience watched. Despite his oil fortune, Manges missed paydays so often that Head Coach Bates quit, or was fired, depending on your point of view. Bates gave an ultimatum of sorts to the front office, making it clear that he would not take the team on the field if players had not been paid.

But the normally upbeat Bates made no progress when it came to the missing paychecks. None of the Gunslingers players received pay the last six games of the season. Players later sued to get their money, but Manges filed bankruptcy.

In 1985, the USFL folded after an antitrust suit against the NFL failed to get any rewards. It was six years before the Gun-slingers were replaced by yet another team—the San Antonio Riders.

The Riders were part of the World League of American Football. Larry Benson was owner and Tom Landry a minority owner. With Mike Riley as head coach and players such as Jason Garrett, Ricky Blake and Mike Kiselak in the fold, the Alamo Stadium–based Riders still failed to make the 1991 playoffs. For the 1992 season Benson moved the Riders to Bobcat Stadium in San Marcos because beer could not be sold at the San Antonio School District–owned Alamo Stadium. The Riders played one more season before the World League of American Football ceased operations.

San Antonio football great Roger Gill was a player, head coach and team owner.

Since then there have been other attempts to revitalize football in San Antonio, some futile, some impressive. There was the Arena football experiment with the San Antonio Force in 1992, a partnership with the San Antonio Spurs. Despite fair attendance, the Force folded either because they didn't have a place to play for the upcoming 1993 season or because the Spurs front office was spread too thin running both a football and a basketball franchise.

So if not American football, why not Canadian? In January 1993 a Canadian Football League expansion franchise was to debut in San Antonio, but that was dropped when financial woes surfaced. Two years later the CFL got their team with the San Antonio Texans, a CFL franchise that relocated to San Antonio from Sacramento. The Texans, led by quarterback Dave Archer, played in the Alamodome, compiled a 12-6 record and made it to the division championship against the Baltimore Stallions, eventually losing. Later in 1995 several American franchises folded their teams, leaving the Texans as the only American team standing.

Despite local owners' intentions to hang on, the Texans soon followed in the Gunslingers' and Riders' footsteps.

Since 1998 at least four more football teams have blossomed in San Antonio with great enthusiasm, only to be dashed by losing money and having their funding pulled. Other than the local die-hard football fan, few can recall the fleeting exploits of the Stampede, Matadors, Thunder and Coyotes.

In 1999 San Antonio lost a true football giant, a man who meant more to local minor league football than any person—Roger Gill, who lost his two-year battle with Lou Gehrig's disease. As a player, head coach and owner, Gill had his hand in every aspect of local pro football. His efforts to bring an NFL franchise to San Antonio had never wavered. After his football days with Texas Tech were over he had a brief career with the NFL's Philadelphia Eagles in the 1960s, but it was his days with the San Antonio Toros that provided his greatest fame.

Nowadays the local pro football scene has settled on the Dallas Cowboys training camp, at the Alamodome in 2002 and 2003. The camps do come at a price, which caused an uproar when the Cowboys asked for $1 million from the city to hold camp at the dome. The amount was negotiated down to nearly $400,000, but only after much City Council wrangling and a barely favorable 6–5 vote. Time will tell if the agreement will lead to a multiyear partnership and benefit the city.

4. Dribbling to Glory

Basketball is the local sport that garners the most attention from San Antonio fans. As the only major league franchise this city has had, the San Antonio Spurs have established a fervent following, the likes of which had never been seen here before.

San Antonio's first taste of professional basketball came in February 1950, when the Harlem Globetrotters—featuring Goose Tatum, Nat Clifton and Marques Haynes—paid a visit to San Antonio in the first of several decades of barnstorming tours to this city. Other pro and semi-pro basketball teams followed. For instance, Goose Tatum came back with his Harlem Stars to face Bill Spivey and the New York Olympians in front of 2,629 fans at Municipal Auditorium in January 1958.

Before the Spurs came to town, the Minneapolis Lakers held training camp in San Antonio, in September 1959, so that, between training sessions, Lakers Elgin Baylor and Alexander "Boo" Ellis could fulfill their military commitment at San Antonio's Brooke Army Medical Center. As part of the BAMC Comets, Baylor once scored 52 points against a YMCA all-star team at Woodlawn Gym.

With HemisFair '68 and the new HemisFair Arena, it was only a matter of time before the arena attracted sports teams seeking an untapped market. At the time Texas had two pro basketball teams, both ABA members, the Houston Mavericks and the Dallas Chaparrals. Soon they were joined by the NBA's Houston Rockets, who tried to make inroads in San Antonio in 1971.

For their 1971 season, the Rockets scheduled three regular season games at HemisFair Arena, against the Detroit Pistons, Seattle Supersonics and Chicago Bulls. The Rockets drew so well that 14 more games were scheduled the next season in San Antonio, including one exhibition. The key game was the meeting between the Rockets and the defending NBA Champion Los Angeles Lakers featuring Jerry West, Wilt Chamberlain and Head Coach Bill Sharman. With the success from the city's exposure to pro basketball, it wouldn't be long before San Antonio would replace the Rockets with the South Texas Spurs.

Back in the ABA, the Dallas Chaparrals were struggling on and off the basketball court. A move seemed likely if, and only if, the offer was just right. That's when local businessman and stockbroker Angelo Drossos, who had a brief fling as a local boxing promoter, was able to pull together other entrepreneurs to purchase the struggling Dallas franchise. With local car dealer B. J. "Red" McCombs, Drossos was able to lease the Chaparrals for three years with an option to buy.

Formation of the Spurs proved to be a defining moment for both the city and for Drossos. From his initial involvement with the Spurs until 1988, he brought about the ABA/NBA merger, influenced such NBA innovations as the three-point shot and, as part of the NBA board of governors, helped create the NBA salary cap.

Angelo Drossos brought in Red McCombs and other investors to bring a Dallas basketball franchise to San Antonio.

For its inaugural season the Spurs hired a familiar face as head coach, Tom Nissalke, the head coach of the Chaparrals in 1971 who was named ABA Coach of the Year for turning around a dismal team. The Spurs began ABA life with uncertainty. The first games were a novelty, but that quickly wore off, as did attendance. All-Star Rich Jones, a leftover from the Chaparral days, and rookie sensation Swen Nater, who the Spurs got in a trade with the Virginia Squires, helped push the Spurs in the right direction.

But even with up-and-coming point guard James Silas in their midst, something or someone else was going to have to breathe new life into the young franchise and take the Spurs to the next level.

In January 1974 the Spurs worked a deal that brought in from the Virginia Squires a slim 6'7" forward named George Gervin. After initial legal wrangling brought on by ABA Commissioner

Mike Storen ended up in court, the Spurs eventually won their case. The Spurs had their man and eventual savior.

With George "Iceman" Gervin, San Antonio had its first superstar. The scoring machine from Michigan was smooth as honey, and his legendary finger roll had no equal. Gervin would say his best defense was his offense, and he was a perfect fit. The output was evident, especially on the final day of the 1978 season when the NBA scoring title battle came down to Gervin and Denver's David Thompson. Thompson scored 73. Later in the evening Gervin scored 63 points, nosing out Thompson by a hair. Honors were plentiful, whether it was scoring titles, MVP awards or milestones, but the one thing that eluded Gervin was an NBA championship.

Conference finals were as close as Gervin came to that all-important ring, but the memories he brought to the city along with the exposure can never be forgotten.

The Spurs' initial season was indeed successful. The team made it to the playoffs only to lose in the Western Division Semifinals in seven games with a group of budding superstars. The following season there was change in the air when, after posting a 17-10 record, the team replaced Tom Nissalke as head coach with Bob Bass. The Spurs' basketball style changed for good.

By their third season the Spurs had an up-tempo style in place and shooting guard Donnie Freeman lost to free agency. Bass was able to move Gervin to guard position alongside James Silas. The Spurs began to surge. To further bolster their team the Spurs brought in defensive specialist Mike Gale, center Billy Paultz and All-Star Larry Kenon, whom the Spurs exchanged with the New York Nets for Swen Nater.

With playoff appearances in each of the first two seasons, a long playoff run seemed inevitable for the 1976 season despite observers' criticism of the Spurs defense. But that defense was the key in each of their victories in the 1976 playoffs.

But a shot at an ABA championship was not to be, as the New York Nets won a tough seven-game series. The fourth game became the subject of controversy for years to come, as the Nets scored the game's last nine points. When a fight broke out between

George Karl and Brian Taylor with 10:25 left in the second quarter, Net Rich Jones came off the bench and began slugging everyone in sight. The brawl delayed the game for 15 minutes, leaving the momentum clearly in favor of the Nets, who had two of the next three games at Nassau Coliseum.

Later, though, a referee's call proved devastating for the Spurs. With 17 seconds left in the game and the Spurs leading 108-107, George Gervin rebounded a missed shot. Gervin had the ball stripped by Brian Taylor, enabling Julius Erving to pick up the loose ball under the basket and slam it home, being fouled in the process by Coby Dietrick. With Dr. J converting on both free-throws, the Nets won the game 110-108. The series stood at 2-2.

Many observers to this day swear that when Taylor stripped the ball from Gervin he had both feet out of bounds, and that the noncall on Brian Taylor by the referee, Norm Drucker, was the worst they'd ever seen. Also, San Antonio had lost the services of point guard James Silas, who broke his right ankle in game one, and George Gervin played less than 100 percent, favoring the injured right wrist he broke two weeks prior to the playoffs. The loss in game four ended up costing Bob Bass his job.

In the summer of 1976 the long-rumored merger between the NBA and ABA was finally a reality, and the Spurs could say good-bye to the up-and-down ABA. The more established NBA was a stabilizing force for the Spurs.

But with the merger came first-year stipulations, such as no participation in the NBA draft and no television money from national broadcasts. In an upstart division that was home to the likes of Moses Malone, "Pistol Pete" Maravich and Elvin Hayes, the next few seasons were just like the first in the ABA for the Spurs. The only difference was that business was moving at a fever pace. Team sales were up, as was attendance, with television exposure a welcome addition.

Spurs' anticipation in joining the stronger league was disheartened when two-time ABA All-Star James Silas, coming off a magnificent season, injured his knee in the preseason and the Spurs had to enter the NBA without their leader. Silas, known for late-game heroics, was as important as Gervin in the franchise's early years, and his contributions could have been even greater if not for his injuries.

In 1977 the HemisFair Arena roof was raised to accommodate more fans. Play also rose higher, as the Spurs brought home two division titles for the upstart team in a new league. For the 1977–78 season the Spurs again lost Silas to injury but finished with an excellent 52-30 record, only to be outlasted in six playoff games by the Washington Bullets.

By 1979 the Spurs were poised for a run against the team they faced the previous year in the playoffs, the Washington Bullets, led by All-Star Elvin Hayes. Back in the Spurs fold was James Silas. George Gervin remained hot as he captured his second straight NBA scoring title with a 29.6 average. The Spurs bench, which included standouts like Allan Bristow, Louie Dampier, Coby Dietrick and Mike Green, helped immensely in bringing the Spurs to their finest hour in the playoffs. Although the team was broken up after the season, the Spurs made a remarkable run, followed by a more demoralizing downfall.

By dethroning the Dr. J–led Philadelphia 76ers in the semifinals, the smaller Spurs would face a bigger and tougher Bullets squad in the next series. After going up three games to one, the Spurs dropped the next two to set up a controversial game seven which they lost in Maryland, 107-105.

The game was lost on poor shooting, as the Spurs couldn't get their transition game going. They led 103-97 at the 1:53 mark, but the Bullets proceeded to outscore them 10-2 in the final 1:52. Bullet Bobby Dandridge, held in check by Larry Kenon and Spurs double-teaming for most of the series, broke loose with 37 points, including the game winner, with eight seconds left in the ballgame.

Furthermore, Dandridge played great defense on Gervin, who didn't score a single bucket in the last 3:49 of the game. Bench play was also key, as the Washington bench outscored the Spurs bench 28-12.

After a mediocre 1980 season, it was time to break up the team, in a big way. Coach Doug Moe was fired during the season, making way for Stan Albeck. An unhappy Larry Kenon was traded to Chicago. Albeck brought in George Johnson and Dave Corzine to shore up the middle in preparation for the move to the Western Conference's Midwest Division. The Spurs also brought together Kevin Restani, Paul Griffin, Reggie Johnson and Mark Olberding, affectionately known as the "Bruise Brothers" for their tenacious defense and hustle.

The team fashioned a new confidence, yet was still missing a small forward to score at will. The Spurs finished the year with a 52-30 record and found themselves facing the Houston Rockets in the 1981 playoffs. After being up three games to one in the semifinals, the Spurs lost the lead and had to face the Rockets in a deciding game seven. Having dropped two of three home games in the series, the Spurs' chances looked bleak.

In game seven, Houston's Calvin Murphy scored 42 points. Coupled with a disastrous third quarter in which the Spurs were outscored 22-12, that proved too much for San Antonio. The Spurs lost the series and, at season's end, their captain, James Silas, who was traded to Cleveland. Silas had fought an attempted pay cut, feeling he was being singled out for the team's playoff failures.

The Spurs were committed to winning a championship, but were they willing to pay the price? A trade sent guard Ron Brewer and George Johnson to Cleveland for Mike Mitchell. The Spurs had previously tried to get Mitchell due in large part to Albeck's association with the power forward; he had coached Mitchell at Cleveland. The 6'7" Mitchell, nearly automatic with his turnaround jumpers, was the perfect complement to George Gervin.

With Mitchell on board and with emerging point guard Johnny Moore, who took over from Silas as the team's floor leader, the Spurs made it all the way to the 1982 Western Conference finals, only to be swept by the Los Angeles Lakers in four. A more competitive showing in the playoffs would take some retooling in the off-season, most notably to bolster the front line in the likelihood that the Spurs would face the Lakers again.

Artis Gilmore was acquired in a major off-season trade from Chicago for Mark Olberding and Dave Corzine. The deal proved

George Gervin, who brought the Spurs early success, shoots over former New Jersey Rockets' Mike Dunleavy, a former Spur.

valuable, as the Spurs set a franchise record in wins with 53 and became, up to that point, the best Spurs team ever, with all due respect to the 1979 squad. After disposing of the Denver Nuggets in the semifinals, the Spurs faced an injured Lakers team in the Western Conference finals for the second straight season. The Spurs quickly fell behind three games to one.

With a win in Los Angeles, the scene was set for a crucial sixth game back in San Antonio. In a seesaw battle, for most of the game the Lakers bench proved to be the difference, and the Spurs seemed erratic and undisciplined. It came down to Mike Mitchell taking the last shot as the Spurs were down one point with 10 seconds left in the game. For that shot it seemed the whole Lakers team—bench, ball boys and trainer—were in Mitchell's face. Gilmore rebounded, but time ran out before a shot could be put up.

Several factors contributed to the Spurs' demise in game six, such as Los Angeles scoring 22 points off 16 Spurs turnovers. The team defense was good on Los Angeles. Offensively, George Gervin scored six of the last eight Spurs points down the stretch to go along with Gilmore's five rebounds to put San Antonio in position to win. The bench was truly the deciding factor, with Los Angeles outscoring San Antonio 30-10, including 14 points apiece from Michael Cooper and Bob McAdoo.

Thus ended the best season yet for the Spurs. It would turn out to be the last hurrah in many ways for the Spurs and for the city. After a bitter feud with Team President Angelo Drossos, Head Coach Stan Albeck left to coach the New Jersey Nets. His replacement, Mo McHone, was quickly fired after a dismal start, and the team failed to make the playoffs for 1983–84.

Although the Spurs under Cotton Fitzsimmons made the playoffs from 1984 to 1986, the glory years were but a distant memory. Poor draft picks in Alfredrick Hughes, drug problems for some players and bitterness between management and players all contributed to the Spurs' decline in the 1980s. In 1985 George Gervin came off the bench behind a younger Alvin Robertson, the emerging guard who once recorded a quadruple-double in February 1985, but Gervin began missing practices and failing to call with an explanation. Finally he was traded to Chicago for David Greenwood.

Making matters worse, during the 1985–86 season, with the Spurs standing at 18-12, was the loss of point guard Johnny Moore, who fell ill and was hospitalized with what was diagnosed as Desert Fever.

By May 1987, after posting a 28-54 record, the Spurs found themselves in the NBA lottery winning the number one pick. The team picked the player who saved the franchise from the depths of misery: U.S. Naval Academy graduate David Robinson.

The arrival of center David Robinson had to wait two seasons so he could fulfill his military commitment to the Navy. The Spurs were content to wait, though they suffered through some of the worst basketball ever played in San Antonio, winning just 31 and 21 games in those seasons.

The impending arrival meant a new squad of players. Sean Elliott and Willie Anderson were drafted. Key trades brought in power forward Terry Cummings, a scorer badly needed since the Gervin and Mitchell days, and point guard Maurice Cheeks, traded again in February to New York for guard Rod Strickland. During this time—in 1988—Red McCombs bought the team from Angelo Drossos. McCombs had always had an interest in the Spurs. Now, topped off with a new head coach in Larry Brown, fresh from winning the national championship with the Kansas Jayhawks, the Spurs were generating excitement at an all-time high.

In David Robinson's first year the Spurs produced the greatest turnaround in NBA history: a franchise-best 56 wins, welcomed by fans who had labored through some tough seasons. Added to the excitement was the return of an old friend, Johnny Moore, after a two-year absence. Moore had been working out for the upcoming CBA season with Tulsa when the Spurs called. He immediately signed a two-year contract to back up Vernon Maxwell.

In the playoffs, the Spurs made a three-game sweep of the Denver Nuggets and set up a semifinal meeting with the Portland Trailblazers in what would be a classic series.

Having taken all-important game five, 138-132 in double overtime, the Portland Trailblazers were in the driver's seat heading back to San Antonio. But the Spurs frustrated the Trailblazers with their defense, taking game six 112-97. That set up a deciding game in Portland that would be known for the no-look pass.

Fast forward to 2:32 left in regulation, the Spurs leading 97-90. Portland broke out of a shooting slump while San Antonio went into a drought, missing jumpshots and layups. Led by Terry Porter's 36 points, Clyde Drexler's down-the-stretch play and the reappearance of injured center Kevin Duckworth, the Blazers stormed back to take the lead and looked to wind up the series.

The Spurs had other ideas. In overtime and with the score knotted at 103-103 and 28 seconds left, the Spurs had possession of the ball. But Rod Strickland's no-look pass to an unsuspecting Sean Elliott proved fatal, as Blazer Jerome Kersey scooped up the loose ball and threw it down court to a sprinting Clyde Drexler. He dunked the ball but was fouled on a breakaway call, resulting in Portland free throws and possession with 26.2 seconds to go.

After more Portland free throws and a Spurs turnover, the game went to Portland 108-105. The Spurs were led by Willie Anderson's

30 points, Terry Cummings's 27 points and 10 rebounds to go along with David Robinson's 24 points, ending a thrilling but heartbreaking season.

With rumors of the Spurs possibly leaving town swirling all summer long, the 1990-91 season began with promise. The Spurs reeled off a 55-27 record but were surprised in the playoffs by an underdog Golden State Warrior team, bowing out in the first round, three games to one. It would not be the last time the Spurs would end the season on a disappointing note.

The following year, Spurs struggles at midseason were enough to call for coach Larry Brown's dismissal. He was replaced by Vice-President of Basketball Operations Bob Bass. The 1991–92 season was further hampered by injuries to David Robinson's left hand and by Willie Anderson's fractured leg. Both missed the playoffs, and the Spurs were easily swept by the Phoenix Suns in the first round.

The Spurs approached the 1992–93 season, their last at HemisFair Arena, with renewed interest, as they brought in Jerry Tarkanian, a new coach with no NBA experience. The move quickly turned out to be a failure. With the firing of Tarkanian after 20 games, the Spurs hired former Spur John Lucas and were immediately sparked by his energy.

The close to roller-coaster season came to a head in the Western Conference semifinals, as the Spurs lost in the final seconds of game six of their matchup with the Phoenix Suns on a Charles Barkley game-winning shot over David Robinson.

With a move to the Alamodome, the upcoming 1993–94 campaign marked a turning point for the franchise. At the outset, the departures of Avery Johnson and Sean Elliott proved to be a public relations nightmare for the team and for the city. In the aftermath, the arrival in the Sean Elliott trade of Detroit's self-promoting Dennis Rodman brought a new dimension to the team besides the rebounding ability: circus sideshow. In the end, the team ran up a 55-27 record. Critics were silenced for a time. The season saw David Robinson score a franchise record 71 points in the final game, capturing the NBA scoring title by edging out Shaquille O'Neal.

The first-round dismissal of the Spurs in four games by the Utah Jazz, though, was enough to shake up the front office and steer the franchise in another direction.

For 1994–95, after the energetic John Lucas resigned as head coach, former Spurs assistant coach-turned-general manager Gregg Popovich hired a new head coach, the easygoing Bob Hill. The return of Sean Elliott and Avery Johnson proved valuable. The Spurs achieved their best season in franchise history, with a 62-20 record and an MVP year for David Robinson, the first for a Spur. Despite the distractions of Dennis Rodman, the team swept through the first round of the playoffs, defeating the Denver Nuggets and went on to win their semifinal series with the Lakers 4-2.

Then the Spurs found themselves facing the defending NBA Champion Houston Rockets and Hakeem Olajuwon, who had something to prove.

The strange series began with the Spurs not showing up and dropping games one and two, only to show courage in taking the next two in Houston. Just as they did in their series with Utah and then with Phoenix, the Rockets capitalized on the Spurs' missed opportunities. Houston won game five by 21 points, taking a 3-2 series lead and giving momentum to propel them to victory in game six in Houston.

For the Spurs, Avery Johnson was resilient and Sean Elliott was sturdy, but MVP David Robinson struggled and in game six missed free throws and shots down the stretch. No doubt a great opportunity was lost as a lack of intensity from the Spurs reared its ugly head.

The next season San Antonio joined the minor league basketball world, as the Professional Basketball League of Mexico awarded the city a franchise called the San Antonio Tejanos, the league's first U.S. team. The league, begun in 1979, planned a 42-game schedule for the Tejanos, with former Central Catholic High School basketball coach Joe Cortez as head coach.

What followed was a repeat of the Gunslingers' ineptness from years past. Because of a late start in organizing for the season, the team had no permanent home and played in gyms all over San

Antonio, which hurt attendance. Road trips seemed like cross-country treks. Bus trips into Mexico sometimes lasted 20 hours, leaving their road record less than desirable. When it came to the Tejanos roster, the word "fluctuating" comes to mind. No doubt the cause of an ever-changing roster was the pay, set at $2,500 a month.

But by early October, the league owed the Tejanos front office and players more than $23,000 in back pay. The front office kept footing the bill to keep the team afloat amid sinking losses. You knew things had gone from bad to worse when, in early October, the Tejanos left on a road trip, never to be seen or heard from again.

Back to the Spurs. With the disappointing playoff performance still fresh in their mind at the beginning of the 1995–96 season, the Spurs hoped Bob Hill could advance the team further in the playoffs, even make a trip to the NBA finals. The Spurs said good-bye to Dennis Rodman in an October trade that brought in Will Perdue from Chicago.

Things definitely got going when the Spurs went 16-0 for March in the midst of a franchise record 17-game winning streak, though in the playoffs the team found its biggest dilemma. With the Spurs discarding the Phoenix Suns in four games in the first round, dreaded division rival Utah Jazz awaited them in the semifinals. After dropping the first game at the Alamodome, the Spurs had the Jazz in their head. Going back to Utah with the series tied 1-1 was not a good prospect.

Indeed, the road proved disastrous for the Spurs. They lost two games in blowout fashion, returning to San Antonio down 3-1 in the series. The Spurs were victorious 98-87 in game five, but couldn't overcome Utah on the road and dropped game six 108-81.

The 1996–97 Spurs season was one for misery and waste, as many key players fell to injuries. If it wasn't David Robinson's broken foot, it was Charles Smith's knee, Sean Elliott's knee or Chuck Person's back, for which he was lost for the entire year. All the team could fashion was a 20-62 record, the worst in franchise history. Head Coach Bob Hill was replaced by the general manager, Gregg Popovich, in early December. Due to their bad record, the Spurs found themselves in the 1997 NBA lottery with the right to pick first in the NBA draft. Popovich's obvious choice was the Collegiate Player of the Year out of Wake Forest, Tim Duncan.

Tim Duncan made an instant impact on the 1997–98 Spurs. Just as David Robinson had eight years earlier, Duncan led the Spurs to the greatest turnaround in NBA history, with an increase of 36 wins. With the return of a healthy David Robinson, the Spurs made the playoffs, opening up against the Phoenix Suns in the first round. The Spurs defeated the Suns three games to one for a chance at their rivals, who had ousted them from the 1996 playoffs.

Without the home court advantage during this playoff run, the Spurs ran into a Utah itching to return to the NBA finals. Tim Duncan severely sprained his ankle in game two and was lost for the remainder of the series. The Spurs fell to the Jazz four games to one. For his part, Tim Duncan was named NBA Rookie of the Year.

The future looked more promising than before, with a healthy David Robinson back and Coach Gregg Popovich with a full season under his belt. But trouble was brewing as labor rumblings persisted in the NBA. An NBA lockout was enforced, and the Spurs and league would have to wade through negotiations.

An NBA lockout lasting seven months shortened the 1998–99 NBA season to 50 games. The league finally started up in February. With veterans Steve Kerr, Jerome Kersey and Mario Elie joining the team—all were acquired in January—the Spurs looked ready for a run. The February start was something to forget, as they finished the month 6-8. But from then, on the Spurs went on an unbelievable 31-5 run to finish the season and claim the best record in the NBA in the final game of the season. Momentum favored the Spurs. They seemed destined to make the most of it.

The Spurs opened the first playoff round against the Minnesota Timberwolves. After splitting the first two games, the Spurs continued their run by winning seven straight, dispatching the Timberwolves in four games and sweeping through the Los Angeles Lakers, with Shaquille O'Neal and a young Kobe Bryant, in the semifinals. The Spurs earned a Western Conference finals spot against the Portland Trailblazers, a talented team with enormous confidence—so much that their game one loss didn't phase them.

But that would all be dismissed in game two, the greatest game played in San Antonio Spurs history—up to that point, of course.

The date: Memorial Day, 1999. The place: the Alamodome, with 35,000-plus in attendance. For most of his career, Sean Elliott was not one for clutch shooting. Fast forward to the waning moments of game two's fourth quarter. After battling back late in the second half from 18 points down, the Spurs had a chance to win. With 9.9 seconds left in the game, and needing only two to tie, the pass to Sean Elliott was nearly stolen by Stacey Augmon.

As momentum carried him out of bounds, Elliott put up the biggest shot of his career, a three-pointer. The Memorial Day Miracle proved to be the game winner. It propelled the Spurs to finish off the Blazers in games three and four.

Now they faced the Allan Houston, Latrell Sprewell–led New York Knicks, in their first-ever NBA finals appearance. The games were hard fought, but the Spurs prevailed and took a commanding 3-1 series lead, in large part due to tenacious defense and fabulous execution. It was only fitting that a player widely criticized around the NBA as not having a jump shot would take the game-winning jumper from the corner, putting the Spurs ahead 78-77 in the final seconds of game five.

After the 1999 finals, Tim Duncan grips the Spurs' first NBA championship trophy in one hand and, in the other, his NBA finals MVP trophy.

Not a bad showing for Spurs all-time leader in assists Avery Johnson, who'd bounced from team to team and on two different occasions was let go by the Spurs.

After 26 seasons of self-destruction, near misses, bad passes and an endless string of what-if's, the Spurs finally had their NBA championship.

The NBA finals MVP title went to second-year forward Tim Duncan, who averaged 27 points and 14 rebounds in the finals.

The 1999–2000 season was not to be the Spurs' as superstar Tim Duncan went down with a knee injury in April, sidelined for the rest of the season. The loss contributed to the Spurs' early exit from the playoffs, courtesy of the Phoenix Suns. Sean Elliott also missed most of the season, his departure was due to a kidney transplant in August 1999 from his brother Noel. Elliott returned to the basketball court in an emotional game on March 14.

The next two seasons were painful, to say the least, both for the Spurs and for their fans. In both seasons they exited the playoffs thanks to the Los Angeles Lakers. In the 2001 Western Conference finals the Lakers dominated the Spurs and embarrassed them as never before, sweeping the Spurs in four as the Lakers headed to their second NBA championship.

The next year the Spurs made it to Western Conference semifinals, facing the Lakers once again; this time they made the series respectable but still lost the series 4-1 to Los Angeles, the eventual NBA champions.

With the 2002–03 campaign approaching, the Spurs were getting younger and building a nice group of players around Tim Duncan. Gone was one-year wonder Derek Anderson. Sean Elliott retired. Avery Johnson left unceremoniously. Malik Rose came into his own, as did three-point specialist Bruce Bowen. The team also saw the emergence of point guard Tony Parker and little-known Stephen Jackson, and the exciting play of Manu Ginobili.

The impending retirement of David Robinson put them in place for a big free-agent signing in the off-season; plus they had a new arena—the SBC Center.

The Spurs started in not-so-spectacular fashion, but, as NBA seasons go, that's par for any season. Just as before, they embarked on a long road trip in February. But what came of this trip was a turnaround for the club, an NBA record eight consecutive road wins over teams like Portland, Sacramento and the Lakers.

The team was led by none other than reigning MVP Tim Duncan, and it seemed they were ready to make waves in the playoffs. But they would have to go through the Los Angeles Lakers to come out of the West.

After securing the best record in the NBA (60-22) the Spurs had home court advantage throughout the playoffs and a date with the Phoenix Suns in the first round. Phoenix, led by Stephon Marbury and rookie sensation Amare Stoudemire, gave the Spurs trouble during the regular season. Causing fits for the young Tony Parker, Marbury was the key to the Suns' contention early on in the series. Later, an injury forced Marbury to take them only so far, as the Spurs held on to take the series in six games. Stephen Jackson's 21 points in game six proved valuable as someone other than Tim Duncan stepped up. The Spurs won 87-85.

Next up: defending NBA champion Los Angeles Lakers, and the memories of their recent playoff struggles.

In game five, with the series standing at two games apiece, the Lakers rallied from 25 down, outscoring the Spurs 30–16 in the final period to nearly steal a victory. But Robert Horry's three-point attempt at the buzzer missed, and the Spurs walked off with a three games to two series lead. It seemed the air had gone out of the Lakers sails. In dominating fashion the Spurs eliminated the Lakers 110-82 in Los Angeles. Led by Tim Duncan's 37 points, the Spurs had only to look within their own state for their next opponent, the Dallas Mavericks.

Taking a 3-2 lead into game six, the road-tested Spurs seemed desperate for a spark to lift them out of the cellar. That came when trusty veteran Steve Kerr lifted them with his four three-pointers in the third quarter, erasing a 15-point deficit while an ailing Tony Parker and an ineffective Tim Duncan cheered. David Robinson and the rest of the Spurs bench could hardly contain themselves as they advanced to the NBA finals with a 90-78 win over Dallas.

With the New Jersey Nets as their opponents in the NBA finals, the matchup showcased two of the game's best players: Tim Duncan and Jason Kidd. But it was Tim Duncan who dominated in game one, scoring 32 points and pulling down 20 rebounds as he led the Spurs to a 101–89 victory, snapping the Nets' 10-game postseason winning streak.

The Spurs put away the Nets in a decisive third quarter, when the Spurs outscored their opponents 32-17 to break open a tight game. Defense was the key, as a rejuvenated David Robinson helped the Spurs block 12 Nets shots and effectively stop the Nets' running game courtesy of their zone defense. In the intriguing matchup between Tony Parker and Jason Kidd, Parker outplayed Kidd.

In game two the Nets came back behind 30 points from Jason Kidd and took the game 87-85. Add to that Dikembe Mutombo's insertion into the Nets' rotation to hold Tim Duncan in check and the series was tied 1-1.

Poor free throw shooting and turnovers resumed in New Jersey. The Spurs won ugly in a low-scoring game, 84–79, to take a 2–1 series lead in game three. A 14-3 fourth quarter run put away the Nets as the Spurs were led by 26 points from Tony Parker and two important plays down the stretch by Manu Ginobili that preserved the Spurs victory.

The story in game four was the Nets' 77-76 victory, tying the series at two games apiece despite blowing a 15-point lead, shooting 36 percent and not scoring a single basket in the final minutes of the game. Tim Duncan and David Robinson provided much of the offense, but Tony Parker, Malik Rose, Stephen Jackson and Bruce Bowen combined to shoot 4 for 39, and that was the ballgame.

The Spurs moved closer to realizing their goal in game five, as TIm Duncan led the way with 29 points and 17 rebounds to go along with Steve Kerr's two key buckets in the fourth quarter; they took a 93-83 win over New Jersey. It was a repeat performance in some ways for Steve Kerr, as he came off the bench once again to spark the Spurs in game five. His play was not as dramatic as his Western Conference finals play, but it was equally effective in propelling the Spurs to a 3-2 series lead.

Falling short of a quadruple double, Tim Duncan was the difference in game six, as he had been since joining the Spurs franchise. The Spurs' 88-77 win included a fourth-quarter run that reached 19 straight points, despite their trailing for virtually the entire game. For his 21 points, 20 rebounds and 10 assists performance, Duncan was named the NBA finals MVP. David Robinson,

The Spurs are still jubilant after their 88-77 victory in game six in San Antonio's SBC Center, in June 2003. Those who made the picture are, from left, standing, coach Mike Brown, Danny Ferry, Malik Rose, Steve Smith, Tim Duncan (with his second MVP trophy), coaching staffer Chris White, coach Bremand McClinton, Carolyn Carlesimo, assistant coach P. J. Carlesimo (holding Kyle Peter), coach Mike Brungardt;

Seated are Spurs chairman Peter Holt and his wife Julianna Holt, Bruce Bowen, Kevin Willis, David Robinson (with the team trophy), Tony Parker, Stephen Jackson, Speedy Claxton and Manu Ginobili.

in his last game, gave it everything he had, coming up with 13 points and 17 rebounds. One more who deserves credit is Head Coach Gregg Popovich, whose handling of players shaped this team into a stalwart bunch.

But, as Popovich said, the championship wouldn't have occurred except for one thing: San Antonio had the greatest guys in the world.

5. The Ice Wars

Who would have thought that ice hockey would thrive in a South Texas city?

It was in the late 1920s and early 30s that a team called the San Antonio Rangers, played with much success. Led by player-manager Jim Riley, the team won state championships in the South Texas Ice Hockey League from 1929 to 1933 and in 1936. Along with the Rangers, the San Antonio Blackhawks and the San Antonio Americans teams played at the San Pedro Iceland rink in 1931.

Quality of teams and play might not have been on par with today's San Antonio Rampage, but they were the pioneers in hockey at a time when sports of all kinds were starting all over town.

Although efforts began in the 1930s to bring quality minor league hockey to San Antonio, the city would have to wait until 1994, when the Central Hockey League and team owner Horn Chen came calling.

Named the San Antonio Iguanas, this team would play at Freeman Coliseum, not the ideal facility but the only venue that could be fitted for ice hockey. The Central Hockey League's Iguanas brought a sense of closeness among its players and fans that quickly added to the team's appeal. By the fall of 1994, Iguanas marketing was capitalizing successfully on a good first season. Five games into the season, however, Head Coach Bill Goldsworthy, a former NHL player with the Minnesota North Stars, was hospitalized with an illness that turned out to be HIV.

For several games the team struggled, but in came a man that would prove so valuable to ice hockey in this city that his contributions are still being felt today: John Torchetti.

Installed as head coach, Torchetti guided the Iguanas into the league championship round against the Oklahoma City Blazers. With centers Paul Jackson and Brian Shantz leading the way, the

Iguanas opened the series on the road, but the Blazers made an overtime comeback to win in game one and went on to a 3-1 series lead. Behind Iguana Dale Henry's hat trick in game five, however, the Iguanas became more focused and determined, winning 6-4.

Before a sellout crowd of more than 9,300, the Iguanas took game six 5-4 on a Trevor Buchanan wild slapshot in overtime, forcing a seventh game back in Oklahoma City. There the Blazers jumped to an early lead and never looked back, winning the game 4-2 and the championship. John Torchetti ultimately was named Coach of the Year and Paul Jackson was the Most Valuable Player.

The ice hockey phenomenon brought another hockey team to San Antonio in 1996—the San Antonio Dragons of the International Hockey League. They relocated from Peoria, Illinois, where they were the Rivermen. Not only did the two teams have to fight to corner the hockey market in San Antonio; they had to share the same ice rink at Freeman Coliseum. Both had to move out each February for the annual Stock Show and Rodeo.

With the promise of a better brand of play, the Dragons counted on President Jim Goodman, who had been general manager of the Iguanas in 1994. Like the Iguanas before them, the Dragons fielded a good team, but the local hockey scene was dubbed the Ice War. While the Iguanas were second in the CHL in attendance during their first two seasons, arrival of the Dragons pushed the Iguanas to the bottom during 1996–97.

The Iguanas became the Ice War's first casualty, ceasing operations after the Coliseum Advisory Board canceled their five-year contract in a dispute with the Central Hockey League over the Iguanas' profit potential. The matter went to district court.

With the ice to themselves, the Dragons replaced Jim Goodman as president with Craig Jenkins, former marketing whiz with the Western Professional Hockey League. They lowered ticket prices, but the team fell near the bottom in league attendance and suffered serious financial losses. After the 1997–98 season—their second—the Dragons folded and were purchased from Don Levin by former Iguanas owner Horn Chen, who resold them to Missions owner Dave Elmore. The Iguanas were reborn in August 1998.

Rampage Right Wing Denis Shvidki moves the puck down the court.

Again the Iguanas were part of the Central Hockey League and were led by familiar players Paul Jackson and Brian Shantz. But several events soon sealed their demise: their lease at Freeman Coliseum expired at the end of the CHL playoffs and the Spurs relocated an inactive Louisville franchise to play in the SBC Center, the Spurs' newly built home venue next to Freeman Coliseum. When talks over use of the Alamodome broke down, the embittered Iguanas suspended operations after the 2001–02 season.

With the birth of the new San Antonio Rampage they became an affiliate of the NHL's Florida Panthers, who ran day-to-day decisions while the Spurs handled the business side and sponsored an effective marketing campaign. The Rampage also benefited from a new training facility—the Northwoods Ice Center, which is open to the public.

Halfway through their initial season the Rampage lost their mentor, Head Coach John Torchetti, who was called up to the Florida Panthers to be an assistant coach. With the likes of centers Mike Green and Jeff Toms, the Rampage made it to the 2003 playoffs, though they lost in a three-game sweep courtesy of the Norfolk Admirals.

6. In the Ring

Since the late nineteenth century, San Antonio has been a proving ground for professional boxers. In 1882, after his victory over Paddy Ryan, John L. Sullivan himself toured San Antonio, offering $100 to anyone who could last four rounds in the ring with him at the old Turner Hall, on the present site of the Empire Theater. Sullivan returned in 1905 for a four-round exhibition with Jake Kilrain during San Antonio's International Fair.

World champion Jim Corbett trained in San Antonio in 1896, and put on an exhibition at Alamo Plaza's Grand Opera House, sparring with boxers Jim Daley and Steve O'Donnell to prepare for his upcoming fight with Bob Fitzsimmons. Corbett trained at the old Jockey Club grounds, now part of Brackenridge Park's golf course. Bob Fitzsimmons came through a week after Corbett, also staging exhibitions at the Grand Opera House.

In the 1920s the pugilistic scene hit its stride with the likes of local fighters Chuck Burns, Navy heavyweight Champ Clark and promoter Jack Shelton, himself a former boxer, who at Beethoven Hall staged successful fight cards that turned out huge crowds. One of Shelton's stable of fighters was the lightweight Kid Pancho (Francisco Mendoza), who fought off the likes of Johnny McCoy and Newsboy Brown and later worked at the *San Antonio Express*.

There would be more boxing exhibitions in San Antonio, such as Young Stribling's knockout of local favorite Jack League in the mid-1920s. Brought in by promoter Jack Shelton, Jack Dempsey made an exhibition appearance in September 1925 at League Park, where he faced four sparring partners before a crowd of 5,000. The great Max Schmeling followed with an exhibition at Beethoven Hall, brought in by promoter Eddie Vogt early in March 1931.

The 1930s was a down time for San Antonio boxing, with promoters starting up and closing with regularity and with no true local boxing star for fans to get behind. Despite Sunday labor laws, promoter Bob Warren thought that if theaters could operate without punishment so could boxing matches. Texas Governor Ross Sterling disagreed, shut down Warren's operation and threatened him with the Texas Rangers if he reopened.

In the meantime another boxing champion made a stop in San Antonio—none other than Joe Louis. The Brown Bomber staged an exhibition in March 1937 that drew a crowd of black and white spectators. During the war years it wasn't uncommon to see Fritzie Zivic draw several thousand fans at military bases around town. A record fight card was the night in 1944 when Fritzie Zivic took on Kid Azteca in a Bill Davee promotion, bringing in about $9,000 at the gate, a big sum in those days.

Another boxing boom came after the war with the rise of such young boxers as Jimmy Curl, Tony Elizondo and Bobby Dykes. Throughout his career Dykes fought seven world champions, missing becoming one himself by one point. Dykes, who had a great left jab, began his boxing career in a pool hall encounter. He moved from San Antonio to Miami in 1948.

One often overlooked event took place in September 1948, when Don Albert Dominique became the first black licensed boxing promoter in San Antonio. His first fight card, showcasing only black boxers, drew about 250 people to Municipal Auditorium.

At the beginning of the 1950s there was good reason to be a boxing fan. Native son Bobby Dykes went 10 rounds before losing to welterweight champion Sugar Ray Robinson in a nontitle bout in November 1950 in Chicago. Later he also went 10 rounds before losing to Willie Pastrano. Dykes went for the world welterweight title against champion Kid Gavilan in February 1952, but the fight ended in a split-decision in favor of Gavilan. It was the first time a native San Antonian did so and the first time black and white boxers were allowed to fight each other in Florida.

In February 1955 San Antonio native Sporty Harvey became the first black boxer to face a white boxer in Texas when he fought Buddy Turman in Dallas. San Antonio got to see its first female bout when promoter Jimmie Scaramozi staged the Barbara Buttrick vs. Phyllis Kugler fight in October 1957. The flop of a show drew 731 spectators, and the Texas Athletic Commission canceled the tour over alleged weight differences.

In other memorable San Antonio fights of the 1950s, reigning world champion Ezzard Charles staged an exhibition as part of a March of Dimes fund-raiser in January 1951. Four months later, promoter Bill Davee's fight card turned into a circus when Jackie Blair won a decision over Lauro Salas in front of a San Antonio crowd that became so upset after the decision was announced that a riot broke out. Also notable was the 1959 fight between Gene Fullmer and Milo Savage.

San Antonio's boxing attendance record of 4,700, set with the May 1955 fight between Raul Macias and Baby Moe Mario, stood until March 1960, when the José Becerra–Ward Yee bout packed Freeman Coliseum with 8,000 fans. Later in the decade came such notable fighters as Lefty Barrera, Porfirio Zamora and Oscar Albarado. A highlight was the July 1967 Jesus Pimentel–Mimun Ben-Ali fight, in which Pimentel TKO'd his way to victory. Ruben Olivares also took by TKO his March 1970 bout with Romy Guelas.

"The Greatest" made it to San Antonio in October of 1972, as promoter Joe Morales brought "The Muhammad Ali Boxing Show" to Municipal Auditorium. Ali faced four fighters in exhibition bouts. Elmo Henderson was added as a late entry when in a workout prior to the event he boasted that he could whip Ali. Muhammad Ali received $7,200 out of $16,000 in gate receipts.

In March 1978 came San Antonio's first staging of a world title fight, a bout between Jorge Lujan and Roberto Ruvaldino with 9,500 in attendance.

The decade also saw the likes of Terry Krueger and one fighter who would capture the hearts of fans around town like none before—Mike Ayala.

Mike Ayala was the oldest of the four boxing sons of trainer Tony Ayala Sr., which included Sammy, Tony Jr. and Paulie. He had his first fight at age six. By 1975 the three-time Golden Gloves Champion represented the United States in the 1976 Olympics. In 1976 he reeled off an impressive 15-0 record. In his first three years as a pro he made about $90,000 and won the NABF Bantamweight Championship by defeating Cesar Deciga in January 1977.

However, amid the rumors of drug use, Ayala defended his title in May against Rodolfo Martinez, a former world bantamweight champion. Ayala's demons stole his fervor, and he lost the title. Later he was arrested for shooting boxing stable mate Gilbert Galvan. He pleaded guilty to aggravated assault and received a 10-year probated sentence.

Ayala's comeback began in March 1978 with a title fight against Ronnie McGarvey. He knocked out the top featherweight contender in 56 seconds. But in June 1979 in the newly-renovated San Fernando Gymnasium cane Ayala's challenge to WBC Featherweight Champion Danny Lopez, who had a 40-3 record with 38 KOs. Ayala had trained for three months for the fight. It was televised by CBS in front of 12,952 fans.

The fight had everything—drama, controversy and, of course, great boxing. Ayala fought mostly on the ropes rather than keeping Lopez moving, which gave the hard-hitting champion a chance to wear down the challenger with jabs. The seventh round proved to be the turning point for Lopez, as Ayala's nose started to bleed after being knocked to the ring floor for the first time. Lopez used a right upper cut that caused Ayala's eye to swell in the 13th round.

Lopez's devastating right punches finally knocked out Ayala in the 15th round.

In the 1980s the Ayala name still dominated the local boxing scene with the addition of Sammy and Tony Ayala Jr. Veteran promoter Tony Padilla was still putting on fight cards, but a new breed of fighters and managers was taking shape. Emerging were boxers who would rewrite the record books, fighters like John Michael Johnson, "Jesse" James Leija and Robert Quiroga.

To the delight of local boxing fans, in April 1990 Robert Quiroga, who held the USBA superflyweight title, became the first native San Antonian to win a world championship when he defeated Juan Polo Perez for the IBF junior bantamweight title.

Quiroga first caught the eye of the boxing world on the undercard of the 1988 WBA flyweight championship fight in San

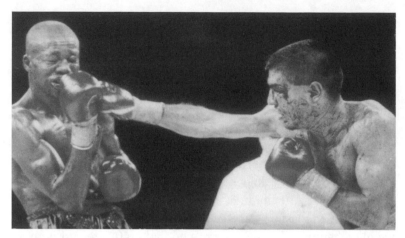

Robert Quiroga jabs at Kid Akeem in 1991 in successfully defending his junior bantamweight crown, the first world boxing title won by a San Antonian.

Antonio between Fidel Bassa and Raymond Medel. With the Perez fight, Quiroga (14-0) was fighting outside San Antonio for the first time. Perez (28-5-2) was so much the aggressor that Quiroga was cut late in the twelfth round. But Quiroga, in the best shape of his career, Quiroga landed most of the better punches, wearing down Perez and taking a unanimous decision for the championship.

Fourteen months later, in his first hometown defense, Quiroga was fighting challenger Kid Akeem Anifowoshe, the better known. NABF champion Kid Akeem boasted a 23-0 record with 18 KOs, but Quiroga was the favorite.

What turned out to be the biggest fight since the Ayala–Lopez bout of 1979—some call it the greatest boxing match ever in San Antonio—was also the bloodiest battle ever witnessed locally. Quiroga was triumphant, and retained his IBF championship by unanimous decision. Kid Akeem congratulated Quiroga, collapsed in his corner and fell into a coma, eventually dying from his injuries. Quiroga, who had to wait an hour before seeing any media or family in his dressing room, also had to be hospitalized.

Quiroga was prone to facial cuts, a factor five title defenses later in January 1993 in his dropping the title to Julio Cesar Borboa. A 1995 comeback try after a two-year layoff was unsuccessful.

Another local championship boxer in the 1990s was "Jesse" James Leija, who won the WBC super featherweight title in 1994 in Las Vegas. Leija (27-0-2) faced veteran Azumah Nelson (37-3-2), whom he had fought to a draw in San Antonio the previous year when Leija's laid-back approach in later rounds cost him the bout.

This time, however, things were different, as Leija took the fight to Azumah Nelson in every round. Time and again the veteran could not land any punches, and in the final round Leija gained a unanimous decision. It turned out to be the best fight of his 16-year career. By 2003 Leija was still boxing, showing that class and dedication can endure.

In 1993 Don King came calling with a super fight card that crammed the Alamodome—in its first year of operation—with 63,000 spectators. In the ring that September night were Terry Norris, defeating Joe Gatti by knockout; Jesse James Leija, battling Azumah Nelson to a controversial draw for the WBC super featherweight title; and the main event, which saw Julio Cesar Chavez taking Pernell Whitaker to a controversial draw for the WBC welterweight title.

A devastating boxer less remembered than the highly publicized Ayala or the glorious James Leija is John Michael Johnson, who retired in 2002 to finish his career with a 30-9 record that included 23 knockouts.

The San Antonio native's crowning achievement came in 1994 when he TKO'd Junior Jones in 11 rounds for the WBA bantamweight championship. Going into that fight, underdog Johnson (17-4) was facing 10-1 odds against the 32-0 defending bantamweight champion. Johnson had trained relentlessly under Tony Ayala Sr. The hard work and preparation paid off, as during the fight Johnson was never really hurt. The critical moment came in the eleventh round, when Johnson unleashed an assault that included a blistering right that sent Jones to the floor and a referee's call for a stoppage.

Another notable fight at the Alamodome came in June 1997, when a crowd of 11,500 saw boxers Floyd Mayweather, James Leija and headliner Oscar De La Hoya, who knocked out David

Kamau in two rounds to retain the WBC welterweight belt, headline a much needed boxing card to breathe life into a San Antonio boxing scene that was on life support after very few attractive boxing shows were staged for much of 1996.

Though gone are the days of Willard Brown and Tracy Cox, Bobby Dykes, Tony Padilla, Leonard Zuniga, Lefty Barrera, Robert Quiroga and Mike Ayala, what remains is nothing short of exceptional, with the likes of the graceful Oscar Diaz and Erik Rodriguez and even the veteran James Leija.

7. Baseball Facts and Figures

Teams

1888
(team unnamed)
1st team disbanded May 24 due to finances; 2nd team replaced Austin, withdrew Aug. 23.
Record: 1st team 6-28 .176; 2nd team 14-11 .560
Manager: 1st team John Cavanaugh, Robert Rose; 2nd team John McCloskey
Ballpark: Muth's Park
President: 1st team Peter Shields, 2nd team John McCloskey

1892
(team unnamed)
Classification: B
Record: 11-20 .355
Manager: Lou Sylvester
Ballpark: San Pedro Park
President: Lou Sylvester

1895
Missionaries
Team disbanded Aug. 7 due to finances.
Classification: B
Record: 21-72 .226
Manager: William Clare out Apr.l 28 (1-8), George Reese Ap.l 29-May 20 (2-18), George Watkins May 21-Jun. 8 (5-12), Red Cox Jun. 9-Jun. 15 (1-6), J.C. Sherry Jun. 16-Jul. 9 (7-12), Gus Land in Jul. 10 (5-16)
Ballpark: San Pedro Park
President: Jones Irvine, William Caperton, Ford Dix.

1896
Bronchos
Classification: C
Record: 57-71 .445
Manager: Dan Crotty out May 29 (14-23),

Mike Lawrence May 30-Aug. 14 (31-40), Mike O'Connor in Aug. 15 (12-8)
Ballpark: San Pedro Park
President: Peter Brophy, James Nolan, George Eichlitz

1897
Bronchos
Texas League co-champions with Galveston; dropped by league to keep an even number of teams after Austin franchise withdrew.
Classification: C
Record: 68-44 .607
Manager: Mike O'Connor
Ballpark: San Pedro Park
President: George Hines, Charlie Weber

1898
Bronchos
Classification: C
Record: 8-19 .296
Manager: Tom Farley out Apr. 11 (2-0), Arthur Rutherford Apr. 12-Apr. 29 (4-14), Frank "Kid☐" Fear inApr. 30 (2-5).
Ballpark: San Pedro Park
President: Louis Welton, Louis Heuermann

1899
Bronchos
Classification: C
Record: 35-40 .467
Manager: Pete Weckbecker out Jun. 22 (30-35), Win Clark Jun. 23-Jun. 25 (0-3), Charlie Weber in Jun. 26 (5-2).
Ballpark: San Pedro Park
President: Louis Heuermann, Fred Dewey

1903
Mustangs
South Texas League champions

Classification: C
Record: 69-54 .561
Manager: Wade Moore
Ballpark: San Pedro Park
President: Wade Moore
Playoffs: San Antonio 7 Galveston 2;
remainder of series cancelled due to
poor attendance

1904
Mustangs
South Texas League
Classification: D to C in Jul.
Manager: Wade Moore out May 17 (4-14),
Ellis Hardy May 18-May 20 (1-2),
Charles Blackburn in May 21 (27-72).
Record: 32-88 .267
Ballpark: San Pedro Park
President: Wade Moore, Charles
Blackburn

1905
Warriors
South Texas League
Classification: D
Record: 69-60 .535
Manager: Bill Morrow out Jun. 1 (9-18),
Walter Morris Jun. 2-Aug. 14 (45-32),
George Page in Aug. 15 (15-10).
Ballpark: San Pedro Park
President: Charles Blackburn, Morris
Block

1906
Bronchos
South Texas League
Classification: C
Record: 57-70 .449
Manager: Bill Alexander out Aug. 4 (44-52),
George Page Aug. 5-Aug. 7 (1-2), Ike
Pendleton in Aug. 8 (12-16).
Ballpark: Electric Park
President: Morris Block

1907
Bronchos
Classification: C
Record: 81-58 .583
Manager: Sam LaRoque out Jul. 25 (53-
41), Pat Newnam in Jul. 26 (28-17).
Ballpark: Electric Park
President: Morris Block

Black Bronchos
Champions of the South
Record: 13-4 .765
Manager: unk.
League: unk.
Ballpark: Electric Park
Owner: Charlie Bellinger
Playoffs: San Antonio 4 Birmingham
Giants 1

1908
Bronchos
Texas League champions
Record: 95-48 .664
Manager: George Leidy out Aug. 16 (74-
44), Pat Newnam Aug. 17-Aug. 21 (3-
2), George Leidy in Aug. 22 (18-2).
Ballpark: Electric Park
President: Morris Block

Black Bronchos
**State champions, champions of the
South**
Record: 35-8 .814
Manager: unk.
League: unk.
Ballpark: Electric Park
Owner: Charlie Bellinger
Playoffs: San Antonio 4 Dallas 3; San
Antonio 4 Birmingham Giants 3

1909
Bronchos
Record: 76-63 .547
Manager: George Leidy
Classification: C
Ballpark: Electric Park
President: Morris Block

Black Bronchos
Record: 26-8 .765
Manager: unk.
League: unk.
Ballpark: Electric Park
Owner: Charlie Bellinger
Playoffs: San Antonio vs Houston; results
of state championship series unknown

1910
Bronchos
Record: 74-62 .544
Manager: George Leidy

Classification: C
Ballpark: Electric Park
President: Morris Block

1911
Bronchos
Record: 77-68 .531
Manager: George Leidy
Classification: B
Ballpark: Electric Park
President: Morris Block

1912
Bronchos
Record: 84-57 .596
Manager: George Leidy out Jul. 19 (59-39), Frank Metz in Jul. 20 (25-18)
Classification: B
Ballpark: Electric Park
President: Morris Block

1913
Bronchos
Record: 74-78 .487
Manager: George Stinson
Classification: B
Ballpark: Block Stadium
President: Morris Block

1914
Bronchos
Record: 46-103 .309
Manager: Clyde Goodwin out May 22 (14-27), Dred Cavender May 23-Aug. 1 (28-46), John Kibler in Aug. 2 (4-30).
Classification: B
Ballpark: Block Stadium
President: Morris Block

1915
Bronchos
Record: 81-67 .547
Manager: George Leidy
Classification: B
Ballpark: League Park
President: Harry Benson

1916
Bronchos
Record: 66-79 .455
Manager: George Leidy out Jun. 27 (35-40), Jack Love Jun. 28-Jun. 29 (0-1),

Dolly Stark Jun. 30-Jul. 30 (17-13), Harry Stewart in Jul. 31 (14-25)
Classification: B
Ballpark: League Park
President: Harry Benson

1917
Bronchos
Record: 76-89 .461
Manager: Charley O'Leary out Jun. 8 (27-39), Clay Perry in Jun. 9 (49-50).
Classification: B
Ballpark: League Park
President: Harry Benson

1918
Bronchos
Record: 43-45 .489
Manager: Clay Perry
Classification: B
Ballpark: League Park
President: Harry Benson

Black Bronchos
Record: 0-1 .000
Manager: unk.
League: unk.
Ballpark: unk.
Owner: unk.

1919
Bronchos
Record: 60-89 .403
Manager: Mique Finn
Classification: B
Ballpark: League Park
President: Harry Benson

Black Aces
Record: 33-9 .786
Manager: unk.
League: unk.
Ballpark: League Park
Owner: ? Taylor, S.J. Moore
Playoffs: San Antonio led state championship series over Dallas 2-1, other results unknown.

1920
Bears
Record: 79-71 .527
Manager: John Nee

Classification: B
Ballpark: League Park
President: Harry Benson

Black Aces
Record: 41-18 .695
Manager: unk.
League: Texas Negro League
Ballpark: League Park
Owners: S.C. Perkins and J.J. Maclin

1921
Bears
Record: 60-98 .380
Manager: John Nee
Classification: A
Ballpark: League Park
President: Harry Benson

1922
Bears
Record: 76-79 .490
Manager: Hub Northen
Classification: A
Ballpark: League Park
President: Harry Benson
Attendance: 41,874

1923
Bears
Record: 81-68 .544
Manager: Bob Coleman
Classification: A
Ballpark: League Park
President: Harry Benson
Attendance: 78,783

Black Aces
Record: 2-0 1.000
Manager: unk.
League: Texas Negro League
Ballpark: League Park
Owner: unk.

1924
Bears
Record: 75-75 .500
Manager: Bob Coleman
Classification: A
Ballpark: League Park
President: Harry Benson
Attendance: 88,280

Black Sox
Southwest Texas Baseball Champions
Record: unk.
Manager: unk.
League: unk.
Ballpark: unk.
Owner: unk.

1925
Bears
Record: 81-64 .559
Manager: Bob Coleman
Classification: A
Ballpark: League Park
President: Mrs. Mabel Benson, Harry Ables
Attendance: 94,158

Black Sox
Record: unk.
Manager: unk.
League: unk.
Ballpark: Block Stadium
Owner: unk.

1926
Bears
Record: 86-70 .551
Manager: Carl Mitze
Classification: A
Ballpark: League Park
President: Harry Ables
Attendance: 148,533

1927
Bears
Record: 65-90 .419
Manager: Carl Mitze out Jul. 27 (48-56),
    Bob Couchman-Ray Flaskamper in as
    co-managers Jul. 27 (6-6), Flaskamper
    out Aug. 8, Couchman in as manager
    Aug. 8 (11-28).
Classification: A
Ballpark: League Park
President: Harry Ables
Attendance: 88,403

Black Indians
Record: unk.
Manager: Reuben Jones
League: unk.
Ballpark: unk.
Owner: unk.

1928
Bears
Record: 76-83 .478
Manager: Frank Gibson
Classification: A
Ballpark: League Park
President: Harry Ables
Attendance: 106,517

1929
Indians
Record: 56-106 .346
Manager: William Alexander out Apr. 23
(2-6), Pat Newnam in Apr. 24 (54-100).
Classification: A
Ballpark: League Park
President: Homer Hammond
Attendance: 77,086

Black Indians
Record: 39-12 .765
Manager: William B. Patterson, Sam Irvin
League: Texas-Oklahoma-Louisiana
Negro League
Ballpark: League Park
Owner: Hayes Pendergraph and J.J.
Macklin, George Holley and J.R. Morris

1930
Indians
Record: 60-93 .392
Manager: George Burns
Classification: A
Ballpark: League Park
President: Homer Hammond
Attendance: 59,828

Black Indians
Record: 22-8 .733
Manager: Reuben Jones
League: Texas Negro League/Texas-
Louisiana Negro League
Ballpark: League Park
Owner: unk.

1931
Indians
Record: 66-94 .413
Manager: Claude Robertson
Classification: A
Ballpark: League Park
President: Homer Hammond
Attendance: 55,202

Black Indians
Record: 32-16 .667
Manager: Reuben Jones
League: Texas Negro League/Texas-
Louisiana Negro League
Ballpark: League Park
President: Hayes Pendergraph to May,
then Cullen Taylor with George
Holley appointed business
manager

1932
Indians
Record: 57-91 .385
Manager: Claude Robertson
Classification: A
Ballpark: League Park burned Jun. 18,
played at Eagle Field Jun. 19, then
Tech Field
President: Homer Hammond
Attendance: 31,761

Black Indians
Record: 2-6 .250
Manager: Reuben Jones, George Moore,
Rob Williams
League: unk.
Ballpark: Van Daele Stadium
Owner: George Moore

1933
Missions
Texas League champions
Record: 79-72 .523
Manager: Hank Severeid
Classification: A
Affiliation: St. Louis Browns
Ballpark: Tech Field
President & Business Manager: Lou
McEvoy , Guy Airey
Attendance: 78,363
Playoffs: San Antonio 3 Houston 0; San
Antonio 4 Galveston 2; New Orleans 4
San Antonio 2

Black Missions
Record: 3-5 .375
Manager: Bill Haynes
League: unk.
Ballpark: Van Daele Stadium
Owner: George Moore

1934
Missions
Record: 89-65 .578
Manager: Hank Severeid
Classification: A
Affiliation: St. Louis Browns
Ballpark: Tech Field
President & Business Manager: Lou
    McEvoy, Guy Airey
Attendance: 125,259
Playoffs: San Antonio 3 Beaumont 2
    Galveston 4 San Antonio 2

Black Missions
Record: unk.
Manager: unk.
League: unk.
Ballpark: unk.
Owner: unk.

1935
Missions
Record: 75-84 .472
Manager: Hank Severeid
Classification: A
Affiliation: St. Louis Browns
Ballpark: Tech Field
President & Business Manager: Lou
    McEvoy, Guy Airey
Attendance: 109,665

Black Missions
Record: 1-2 .333
Manager: unk.
League: unk.
Ballpark: Tech Field
Owner: unk.

1936
Missions
Record: 73-77 .487
Manager: Bob Coleman
Classification: A1
Affiliation: St. Louis Browns
Ballpark: Tech Field
President & Business Manager: Lou
    McEvoy, Guy Airey
Attendance: 97,743

Black Missions
Record: 3-2 .600

Manager: Bill Haynes
League: unk.
Ballpark: unk.
Owner: Curtis Johnson

1937
Missions
Record: 85-76 .528
Manager: Zack Taylor
Classification: A1
Affiliation: St. Louis Browns
Ballpark: Tech Field
President & Business Manager: Donald
    Barnes, Guy Airey
Attendance: 141,341
Playoffs: Oklahoma City 3 San Antonio 2

Black Missions
Record: 3-3 .500
Manager: unk.
League: unk.
Ballpark: Tech Field, Van Daele Stadium
Owner: Joe "Junior" Clack

1938
Missions
Record: 93-67 .581
Manager: Zack Taylor
Classification: A1
Affiliation: St. Louis Browns
Ballpark: Tech Field
President & Business Manager: Donald
    Barnes & Guy Airey
Attendance: 136,249
Playoffs: San Antonio 3 Oklahoma City 0
    Beaumont 4 San Antonio 3

Black Missions
Record: 25-6 .806
Manager: Rufus Ligon, L. Hensley
League: unk.
Ballpark: Van Daele Stadium
Owners: Samuel "Cap" Thompson, Clyde
    Gray

1939
Missions
Record: 89-72 .553
Manager: Zack Taylor
Classification: A1
Affiliation: St. Louis Browns

Ballpark: Tech Field
President & Business Manager: Donald
Barnes & Guy Airey
Attendance: 116,416
Playoffs: Dallas 3 San Antonio 2

Black Missions
Record: 20-5 .800 (80-16 .833 by Sept. 15,
unconfirmed)
Manager: unk.
League: unk.
Ballpark: unk.
Owner: Samuel "Cap" Thompson, Clyde
Gray

1940
Missions
Record: 89-72 .553
Manager: Marty McManus
Classification: A1
Affiliation: St. Louis Browns
Ballpark: Tech Field
President & Business Manager: Donald
Barnes & Guy Airey
Attendance: 97,575
Playoffs: Beaumont 3 San Antonio 0

Black Missions
Record: 5-3 .625
Manager: unk.
League: unk.
Ballpark: Tech Field
Owner: Joe "Junior" Clack

1941
Missions
Record: 58-96 .377
Manager: Marty McManus
Classification: A1
Affiliation: St. Louis Browns
Ballpark: Tech Field
President & Business Manager: Donald
Barnes & Guy Airey
Attendance: 34,010

Black Missions
Record: 8-1 .888
Manager: unk.
League: unk.
Ballpark: unk.
Owner: Samuel "Cap" Thompson

1942
Missions
Record: 80-68 .541
Manager: Ralph Winegarner
Classification: A1
Affiliation: St. Louis Browns
Ballpark: Tech Field
President & Business Manager: Donald
Barnes & Guy Airey
Attendance: 66,792
Playoffs: Beaumont 4 San Antonio 2

Black Missions
Record: 7-0 1.000
Manager: Bill Haynes
League: unk.
Ballpark: unk.
Owner: Samuel "Cap" Thompson

1943
Black Missions
Record: 2-0 1.000
Manager: unk.
League: unk.
Ballpark: Tech Field
Owner: unk.

1944
Black Missions
Record: 19-2 .905
Manager: Bill Haynes
League: unk.
Ballpark: Tech Field
Owner: Samuel "Cap" Thompson

1945
Black Missions
Record: 14-6 .700
Manager: Bill Haynes
League: unk.
Ballpark: Tech Field
Owner: Samuel "Cap" Thompson

1946
Missions
Record: 87-65 .572
Manager: Jimmy Adair
Classification: AA
Affiliation: St. Louis Browns
Ballpark: Tech Field
President: Bill Osley

Attendance: 295,103
Playoffs: Dallas 4 San Antonio 1

Black Missions
Record: 4-3 .571
Manager: Bill Haynes
League: unk.
Ballpark: Tech Field
Owners: Samuel "Cap" Thompson, Albert "Naps" Johnson

1947
Missions
Record: 60-94 .390
Manager: Jimmy Adair out May 31 (19-28), Mark Carrola in Jun. 1 (41-66).
Classification: AA
Affiliation: St. Louis Browns
Ballpark: Mission Stadium
President: Bill Osley
Attendance: 152,605

Black Missions
Record: 7-6 .538 (29-6 .829 by November, unconfirmed)
Manager: unk.
League: unk.
Ballpark: Brooksdale Park
Owner: Samuel "Cap" Thompson and Albert "Naps" Johnson

1948
Missions
Record: 75-76 .497
Manager: Gus Mancuso
Classification: AA
Affiliation: St. Louis Browns
Ballpark: Mission Stadium
President: Bill Osley
Attendance: 263,959

Black Missions
Record: 9-3 .750
Manager: Stanley Matthews
League: unk.
Ballpark: Pittman-Sullivan Park, Brooksdale Park, Parish League Park, Cielito Lindo Park
Owner: Samuel "Cap" Thompson, Albert "Naps" Johnson

1949
Missions
Record: 70-83 .458
Manager: Gus Mancuso
Classification: AA
Affiliation: St. Louis Browns
Ballpark: Missions Stadium
President: Bill Osley, died Apr. 3 soon after William Byrd took over as acting president/business manager
Attendance: 225,500

Black Missions
Record: 4-4 .500
Manager: unk.
League: unk.
Ballpark: Brooksdale Park, Pittman-Sullivan Park.
Owner: Samuel "Cap" Thompson

Travelers
Record: unk.
Manager: unk.
League: Texas Negro League
Ballpark: unk.
Owner: unk.

1950
Missions
Texas League champions
Record: 79-75 .513
Manager: Don Heffner
Classification: AA
Affiliation: St. Louis Browns
Ballpark: Mission Stadium
President: Bob Tarleton
Attendance: 180,580
Playoffs: San Antonio 4 Beaumont 0; San Antonio 4 Tulsa 2; San Antonio 4 Nashville 3

1951
Missions
Record: 86-75 .534
Manager: Jo-Jo White
Classification: AA
Affiliation: St. Louis Browns
Ballpark: Mission Stadium
President: Joe McShane
Attendance: 180,577
Playoffs: San Antonio 4 Dallas 3
Houston 4 San Antonio 0

1952
Missions
Record: 79-82 .491
Manager: Jo-Jo White
Classification: AA
Affiliation: St. Louis Browns
Ballpark: Mission Stadium
President: Joe McShane
Attendance: 110,001

1953
Missions
Record: 67-87 .435
Manager: Jimmie Crandall out Jul. 11 (38-
    54), Bill Norman in Jul. 12 (29-33).
Classification: AA
Affiliation: St. Louis Browns
Ballpark: Mission Stadium
General Manager: Stan McIlvaine
Attendance: 98,711

1954
Missions
Record: 78-83 .484
Manager: Don Heffner
Classification: AA
Affiliation: Baltimore Orioles
Ballpark: Mission Stadium
General Manager: Stan McIlvaine
Attendance: 149,065

1955
Missions
Record: 93-68 .578
Manager: Don Heffner
Classification: AA
Affiliation: Baltimore Orioles
Ballpark: Mission Stadium
General Manager: Stan McIlvaine
Attendance: 150,861
Playoffs: Shreveport 4 San Antonio 2

1956
Missions
Record: 76-78 .494
Manager: Joe Schultz Jr.
Classification: AA
Affiliation: Baltimore Orioles
Ballpark: Mission Stadium
General Manager: Stan McIlvaine
Attendance: 100,001

1957
Missions
Record: 76-78 .494
Manager: Joe Schultz Jr.
Classification: AA
Affiliation: Baltimore Orioles
Ballpark: Mission Stadium
General Manager: Marvin Milkes
Attendance: 93,661
Playoffs: Houston 4 San Antonio 3

1958
Missions
Record: 74-79 .484
Manager: Grady Hatton
Classification: AA
Affiliation: Independent
Ballpark: Mission Stadium
General Manager: Marvin Milkes
Attendance: 101,305

1959
Missions
Record: 75-70 .517
Manager: Grady Hatton
Classification: AA
Affiliation: Chicago Cubs
Ballpark: Mission Stadium
General Manager: Marvin Milkes
Attendance: 111,487
Playoffs: San Antonio 2 Victoria 0; Austin
    3 San Antonio 0

1960
Missions
Record: 77-68 .531
Manager: Grady Hatton out Jul. 17 (50-
    42), Lou Klein in Jul. 18 (27-26).
Classification: AA
Affiliation: Chicago Cubs
Ballpark: Mission Stadium
General Manager: Dick King
Attendance: 106,273
Playoffs: Tulsa 3 San Antonio 1

1961
Missions
Texas League co-champions with
    Amarillo
Record: 74-65 .532
Manager: Rip Collins out May 12 (15-15),

Harry Craft May 13-May 30 (12-6),
Bobby Adams May 31-Jul. 2 (15-17),
Rube Walker in Jul. 3 (32-27).
Classification: AA
Affiliation: Chicago Cubs
Ballpark: Mission Stadium
General Manager: Dick King
Attendance: 91,493
Playoffs: San Antonio 3 Tulsa 1; San
    Antonio 3 Austin 0; San Antonio 4
    Veracruz 2

1962
Missions
Record: 68-72 .486
Manager: Walt Dixon
Classification: AA
Affiliation: Chicago Cubs
Ballpark: Mission Stadium
General Manager: Jon Ferraris
Attendance: 101,917

1963
Bullets
Texas League co-champions with Tulsa
Record: 79-61 .564
Manager: Lou Fitzgerald
Classification: AA
Affiliation: Houston Colt .45s
Ballpark: Mission Stadium
General Manager: Jon Ferraris
Attendance: 84,965
Playoffs: San Antonio 3 El Paso 2; Tulsa
    3 San Antonio 1

1964
Bullets
Texas League champions
Record: 85-55 .607
Manager: Lou Fitzgerald
Classification: AA
Affiliation: Houston Colt .45s
Ballpark: Mission Stadium
General Manager: Ward Goodrich
Attendance: 85,808
Playoffs: San Antonio 3 El Paso 1; San
    Antonio 3 Tulsa 1

1968
Missions
Record: 53-86 .381
Manager: Harry Bright

Classification: AA
Affiliation: Chicago Cubs
Ballpark: V. J. Keefe Field
General Manager: Elmer Kosub
Attendance: 40,069

1969
Missions
Record: 51-81 .386
Manager: Jim Marshall
Classification: AA
Affiliation: Chicago Cubs
Ballpark: V. J. Keefe Field
General Manager: Elmer Kosub
Attendance: 38,024

1970
Missions
Record: 67-69 .493
Manager: Jim Marshall
Classification: AA
Affiliation: Chicago Cubs
Ballpark: V. J. Keefe Field
General Manager: Woody Bell
Attendance: 44,271

1971 (Dixie Association)
Missions
Record: 63-77 .450
Manager: Walt Dixon
Classification: AA
Affiliation: Chicago Cubs
Ballpark: V. J. Keefe Field
General Manager: Woody Bell
Attendance: 47,113

1972
Brewers
Record: 53-87 .379
Manager: Mike Roarke out Jun. 5 (18-27),
    Al Widmar in Jun. 6-out Jun. 16 (5-6),
    Jim Walton in Jun. 17 (30-54).
Classification: AA
Affiliation: Milwaukee Brewers
Ballpark: V. J. Keefe Field
General Manager: John Begzos
Attendance: 253,139

1973
Brewers
Record: 82-57 .590
Manager: Tony Pacheco

Classification: AA
Affiliation: Cleveland Indians
Ballpark: V. J. Keefe Field
General Manager: John Begzos
Attendance: 177,197
Playoffs: Memphis 3 San Antonio 2

1974
Brewers
Record: 68-64 .515
Manager: Woody Smith
Classification: AA
Affiliation: Cleveland Indians
Ballpark: V. J. Keefe Field
General Manager: Mike Boyle
Attendance: 143,519

1975
Brewers
Record: 50-85 .370
Manager: Woody Smith
Classification: AA
Affiliation: Cleveland Indians
Ballpark: V. J. Keefe Field
General Manager: Joe Garcia
Attendance: 138,517

1976
Brewers
Record: 63-71 .470
Manager: Marty Martinez
Classification: AA
Affiliation: Texas Rangers
Ballpark: V. J. Keefe Field
General Manager: Bob Drew
Attendance: 60,122

1977
Dodgers
Record: 61-67 .477
Manager: Don LeJohn
Classification: AA
Affiliation: Los Angeles Dodgers
Ballpark: V. J. Keefe Field
General Manager: Wally Moon
Attendance: 53,359

1978
Dodgers
Record: 79-57 .581
Manager: Don LeJohn

Classification: AA
Affiliation: Los Angeles Dodgers
Ballpark: V. J. Keefe Field
General Manager: Wally Moon
Attendance: 74,420

1979
Dodgers
Record: 69-62 .527
Manager: Don LeJohn
Classification: AA
Affiliation: Los Angeles Dodgers
Ballpark: V. J. Keefe Field
General Manager: Wally Moon
Attendance: 63,990
Playoffs: San Antonio 2 Midland 1;
    Arkansas 3 San Antonio 0

1980
Dodgers
Record: 74-62 .544
Manager: Don LeJohn
Classification: AA
Affiliation: Los Angeles Dodgers
Ballpark: V. J. Keefe Field
General Manager: Wally Moon
Attendance: 153,355
Playoffs: San Antonio 2 Amarillo 0;
    Arkansas 3 San Antonio 0

1981
Dodgers
Record: 76-57 .571
Manager: Don LeJohn
Classification: AA
Affiliation: Los Angeles Dodgers
Ballpark: V. J. Keefe Field
General Manager: Bill Pagani
Attendance: 134,668
Playoffs: San Antonio 2 Amarillo 1;
    Jackson 3 San Antonio 0

1982
Dodgers
Record: 68-68 .500
Manager: Don LeJohn
Classification: AA
Affiliation: Los Angeles Dodgers
Ballpark: V. J.Keefe Field
General Manager: Bill Pagani
Attendance: 138,024

1983
Dodgers
Record: 66-70 .485
Manager: Terry Collins out Jun. 28 (36-38), Rick Ollar-Dave Wallace in as co-managers Jun. 29 (30-32).
Classification: AA
Affiliation: Los Angeles Dodgers
Ballpark: V. J. Keefe Field
General Manager: Bill Pagani
Attendance: 100,283

1984
Dodgers
Record: 64-72 .471
Manager: Gary Larocque
Classification: AA
Affiliation: Los Angeles Dodgers
Ballpark: V. J. Keefe Field
General Manager: Bill Pagani
Attendance: 125,542

1985
Dodgers
Record: 59-75 .440
Manager: Gary Larocque
Classification: AA
Affiliation: Los Angeles Dodgers
Ballpark: V. J. Keefe Field
General Manager: Bill Pagani
Attendance: 106,183

1986
Dodgers
Record: 64-71 .474
Manager: Gary Larocque
Classification: AA
Affiliation: Los Angeles Dodgers
Ballpark: V. J. Keefe Field
General Manager: Steve Ford
Attendance: 122,261

1987
Dodgers
Record: 50-86 .368
Manager: Gary Larocque
Classification: AA
Affiliation: Los Angeles Dodgers
Ballpark: V. J. Keefe Field
General Manager: Ethan Blackaby
Attendance: 122,277

1988
Missions
Record: 73-60 .549
Manager: Kevin Kennedy
Classification: AA
Affiliation: Los Angeles Dodgers
Ballpark: V. J. Keefe Field
General Manager: Burl Yarbrough
Attendance: 130,899
Playoffs: El Paso 2 San Antonio 0

1989
Missions
Record: 49-87 .360
Manager: John Shoemaker
Classification: AA
Affiliation: Los Angeles Dodgers
Ballpark: V. J. Keefe Field
General Manager: Burl Yarbrough
Attendance: 158,402

1990
Missions
Record: 78-56 .582
Manager: John Shoemaker
Classification: AA
Affiliation: Los Angeles Dodgers
Ballpark: V. J. Keefe Field
General Manager: Burl Yarbrough
Attendance: 180,931
Playoffs: San Antonio 2 El Paso 1; Shreveport 4 San Antonio 2

1991
Missions
Record: 61-75 .449
Manager: John Shoemaker
Classification: AA
Affiliation: Los Angeles Dodgers
Ballpark: V. J. Keefe Field
General Manager: Burl Yarbrough
Attendance: 185,336

1992
Missions
Record: 62-74 .456
Manager: Jerry Royster
Classification: AA
Affiliation: Los Angeles Dodgers
Ballpark: V. J. Keefe Field
General Manager: Burl Yarbrough
Attendance: 177,365

1993
Missions
Record: 58-76 .433
Manager: Glenn Hoffman
Classification: AA
Affiliation: Los Angeles Dodgers
Ballpark: V. J. Keefe Field
General Manager: Burl Yarbrough
Attendance: 189,251

1994
Missions
Record: 62-74 .456
Manager: Tom Beyers
Classification: AA
Affiliation: Los Angeles Dodgers
Ballpark: Wolff Stadium
General Manager: Burl Yarbrough
Attendance: 411,959

Tejanos
Record: 37-51 .420
Manager: Jose Cruz
Affiliation: Independent
League: Texas-Louisiana League
Ballpark: V. J. Keefe Field
General Manager: Mike Marek
Attendance: 14,408

1995
Missions
Record: 64-72 .471
Manager: John Shelby
Classification: AA
Affiliation: Los Angeles Dodgers
Ballpark: Wolff Stadium
General Manager: Burl Yarbrough
Attendance: 387,090

1996
Missions
Record: 69-70 .496
Manager: John Shelby
Classification: AA
Affiliation: Los Angeles Dodgers
Ballpark: Wolff Stadium
General Manager: Burl Yarbrough
Attendance: 381,001

1997
Texas League Champions
Missions

Record: 84-55 .604
Manager: Ron Roenicke
Classification: AA
Affiliation: Los Angeles Dodgers
Ballpark: Wolff Stadium
General Manager: Burl Yarbrough
Attendance: 336,542
Playoffs: San Antonio 4 Shreveport 3

1998
Missions
Record: 67-73 .479
Manager: Ron Roenicke out Jun. 26 (44-
    37), Lance Parrish in Jun. 27 (23-36).
Classification: AA
Affiliation: Los Angeles Dodgers
Ballpark: Wolff Stadium
General Manager: Dave Oldham
Attendance: 387,715
Playoffs: Wichita 3 San Antonio 2

1999
Missions
Record: 67-73 .479
Manager: Jimmy Johnson
Classification: AA
Affiliation: Los Angeles Dodgers
Ballpark: Wolff Stadium
General Manager: Dave Oldham
Attendance: 318,590

2000
Missions
Record: 64-76 .457
Manager: Rick Burleson
Classification: AA
Affiliation: Los Angeles Dodgers
Ballpark: Wolff Stadium
President: Burl Yarbrough
Attendance: 325,137

2001
Missions
Record: 70-67 .511
Manager: Dave Brundage
Classification: AA
Affiliation: Seattle Mariners
Ballpark: Wolff Stadium
President: Burl Yarbrough
Attendance: 309,113
Playoffs: Round Rock 3 San Antonio 2

2002
Missions
Texas League Champions
Record: 68-72 .486
Manager: Dave Brundage
Classification: AA
Affiliation: Seattle Mariners
Ballpark: Wolff Stadium
President: Burl Yarbrough
Attendance: 316,983
Playoffs: San Antonio 3 Round Rock 2;
    San Antonio 4 Tulsa 3

2003
Missions
Texas League Champions
Record: 88-51 .633
Manager: Dave Brundage
Classification: AA
Affiliation: Seattle Mariners
Ballpark: Wolff Stadium
President: Burl Yarbrough
Attendance: 305,235
Playoffs: San Antonio 4
    Frisco 1

Records, Honors

Division Titles
1903 1st half
1973 Western Division
1979 1st half Western Division
1980 1st half Western Division
1981 1st half Western Division
1988 1st half Western Division
1990 2nd half Western Division
1997 1st & 2nd half Western Division
1998 1st half Western Division
2001 2nd half Western Division
2002 2nd half Western Division
2003 1st & 2nd half Western Division

Leaders in Batting
1896 Mike O'Connor .395 (Denison, San
    Antonio)
1905 Earl Gardner .306
1912 Frank Metz .323
1923 Ike Boone .402
1925 Danny Clark .399
1933 Pid Purdy .358
1934 Chet Morgan .342 (Beaumont/San
    Antonio)
1950 Frank Saucier .343
1981 Steve Sax . 346
1990 Eric Karros . 352
1995 Wilton Guerrero .348

Leaders in Runs Scored
1888 Farmer Weaver 66 (Austin/San
    Antonio)
1908 E.C. Collins 113
1910 Otto McIvor 87

1916 John Baggan 90
1917 John Baggan 102
1923 Ike Boone 134
1938 Sig Gryska 100
1951 Bobby Balcena 114
1971 Billy North 91
1981 Mark Bradley 98
2003 Justin Leone 103

Leaders in Hits
1888 Farmer Weaver 90 (Austin/San
    Antonio)
1912 Frank Metz 171
1920 Eddie Brown 200
1923 Ike Boone 241
1925 Danny Clark 225
1934 Chet Morgan 216 (Beaumont/San
    Antonio)
1936 Debs Garms 203
1939 Johnny Lucadello 182
1990 Eric Karros 179

Leaders in Home Runs
1896 Mike O'Connor 18 (Denison/San
    Antonio)
1908 Pat Newnam 18
1910 George Stinson 11
1911 Frank Metz 22
1912 Frank Metz 21
1917 Roy Leslie 18
1940 Pinky Jorgensen 23
1952 Bud Heslet 31
1960 Layton Ducote 32
1961 Craig Sorensen 27

1964 Chuck Harrison 40
1970 Adrian Garrett 29
1972 Gorman Thomas 26
1981 Greg Brock 32
1984 Ralph Bryant 31
1990 Henry Rodriguez 28
1992 Billy Ashley

Leaders in Runs Batted In

1923 Ike Boone 135
1934 Larry Bettencourt 129
1940 Vern Stephens 97
1951 Jim Dyck 127
1954 Frank Kellert 146
1955 Jim Pisoni 118
1990 Henry Rodriguez 109

Leaders in Stolen Bases

1899 Win Clark 58
1903 Gerald Hayes 91 (Houston/San
  Antonio, league record)
1905 Lew Haidt 51 (Beaumont/San
  Antonio)
1921 Snake Henry 52
1925 Danny Clark 29
1926 Ray Flaskamper 30
1928 Ray Flaskamper 48
1971 Billy North 47
1976 Keith Chauncey 31
1979 Mike Wilson 56
1990 Tom Goodwin 60
1991 Eric Young 70
1999 Mike Metcalfe 57
2002 Jamal Strong 46
2003 Mike Curry 58

Leaders in Pitching–Wins

1903 Orth Thomas 22
1915 Emmett Munsell 25
1926 Tiny Owens 22
1934 Ash Hillin 24
1939 Emil Bildilli 22
1940 Maury Newlin 23
1960 Jack Curtis 19
1968 Archie Reynolds 13
1973 Rick Sawyer 18
1974 Dennis Eckersley 14
1980 Brian Holton 15
1983 Sid Fernandez 13
1984 Tim Meeks 14

1993 Ben Van Ryn 14
1995 Gary Rath 13
2003 Travis Blackley 17

Leaders in Pitching–Strikeouts

1888 Frank Hoffman 231 (Austin/San
  Antonio)
1909 Fred Winchell 260
1910 Harry Ables 325
1913 Dave Davenport 204
1933 Jim Walkup 146
1953 Ryne Duren 212
1962 Harvey Branch 216
1974 Dennis Eckersley 163
1978 Richard Sander 159
1980 Fernando Valenzuela 162
1983 Sid Fernandez 209
1989 Chris Nichting 136
1991 Dennis Springer 138
1999 Eric Gagne 185
2001 Jeff Heaverlo 173
2003 Clint Nageotte 157

Earned Run Average

1942 John Whitehead
1983 Sid Fernandez 2.82
1993 Ben Van Ryn 2.21
1995 Gary Rath 2.77
1999 Eric Gagne 2.63

Saves

1970 Don Nottebart 15
1973 Luis Penalver 20
1978 Dave Patterson 19
1979 Mickey Lashley 12
1981 Orel Hershiser 15
1983 Roberto Alexander 22
1999 Matt Montgomery 26
2003 Jared Hoerman 36

MVPs of All-Star Game

1981 Dale Holman
1983 Sid Fernandez

All-Star Team Selections at Season's End

1933 Cap Crossley, Fabian Kowalik, Pid
  Purdy
1934 Tommy Heath, Ash Hillin, Chet
  Morgan
1935 Earl Caldwell

1936 Debs Garms, Sig Gryska, Lefty Mills
1948 Bill Sommers
1959 Lee Handley
1960 Jack Curtis, Duke Ducote, J.C. Hartman
1962 Don Eaddy
1963 Joe Hoerner, Mike White
1964 Don Bradey, Clint Courtney, Chuck Harrison, Sonny Jackson, Joe Morgan, Leo Posada, Chris Zachary.
1969 Dean Burk, Brock Davis, John Felske, Oscar Gamble.
1970 Adrian Garrett, Pat Jacquez.
1971 Billy North
1972 Gorman Thomas
1973 Joe Azcue, Jim Kern, Duane Kuiper, Jeff Newman, Luis Penalver, Rick Sawyer.
1974 Dennis Eckersley
1976 John Poloni
1978 Mickey Hatcher, Dave Patterson.
1979 Ron Roenicke, Gary Weiss.
1981 Mark Bradley, Dale Holman, Tom Niedenfuer, Rich Rodas, Dave Sax, Steve Sax, Mike Zouras.
1982 Dann Bilardello, Dean Rennicke, Paul Voigt.
1983 Sid Fernandez, R.J. Reynolds.
1984 Ralph Bryant, Tim Meeks, Gilberto Reyes, Joe Vavra.
1985 Jeff Hamilton, Jose Gonzalez, Scott May.
1986 Mike Devereaux, Shawn Hillegas, Tracy Woodson.
1987 Mike Devereaux, Joe Szekely.
1988 Mike Huff, Domingo Michel, Mike Munoz
1989 Carlos Hernandez
1990 Steve Finken, Tom Goodwin, Mike James, Eric Karros, Henry Rodriguez.
1992 Billy Ashley
1993 Rick Gorecki, Ben Van Ryn
1994 Juan Castro
1995 Wilton Guerrero, Oreste Marrero, David Pyc, Gary Rath.
1996 Paul Konerko, Eric Weaver
1997 Kevin Gibbs, J.P. Roberge, Paul LoDuca.
1998 Adrian Beltre, Peter Bergeron, Ted Lilly, Angel Pena.
1999 Eric Gagne, Tony Mota.
2000 Luke Prokopec

2001 Jeff Heaverlo
2002 Craig Anderson
2003 Travis Blackley, Mike Curry, Justin Leone, Jose Lopez, Bobby Madritsch, Clint Nageotte, A.J. Zapp.

Manager of the Year

1973 Tony Pacheco
1997 Ron Roenicke
2003 Dave Brundage

Player of the Year

1940 Bob Muncrief
1951 Jim Dyck
1954 Frank Kellert
1964 Joe Morgan
1981 Steve Sax
1990 Henry Rodriguez
2003 Justin Leone

Pitcher of the Year

1934 Ash Hillin
1951 Bob Turley
1960 Jack Curtis
1964 Chris Zachary
1974 Dennis Eckersley
1983 Sid Fernandez
1993 Ben Van Ryn
1999 Eric Gagne
2003 Travis Blackley

Batting Records

Most Runs in a Game 34 Apr. 12,1981
Most Hits in a Game 32 May 17,1925
Most Home Runs in Game 6 Apr. 8,1925, May 3,1925
Most Games Won 95 1908
Highest Winning Percentage .664 (95-48) 1908
Most Home Games Won 54 1908
Highest Home Winning Percentage .750 (48-16) 1897
Most Road Games Won 41 1908
Highest Road Winning Percentage .621 (41-25) 1908
Most Consecutive Games Won 18 2003
Most Consecutive Home Games Won 15 1973
Most Consecutive Road Games Won 14 2003
Highest Season Attendance 411,959 1994

Largest Game Attendance 12,946 Jun. 1,1962

Longest Game by Innings 26 Jul. 14-16,1988 (league record

Individual Batting Records

Batting Average .402 Ike Boone 1923

Runs 134 Ike Boone 1923

Hits 241 Ike Boone 1923

Doubles 53 Ike Boone 1923

Triples 26 Ike Boone 1923

Home Runs 41 Frank Kellert 1954

RBI'S 146 Frank Kellert 1954

Bases on Balls 115 Bob Caffery 1956

Stolen Bases 70 Eric Young 1991

Longest Batting Streak 35 Games Ike Boone (Jun. 24-Jul. 27,1923)

Most Consecutive Games Played 508 John Baggan (Apr. 8,1915-May 26,1918)

Individual Pitching Records

Wins 25 Emmett Munsell 1915

Losses 26 Richard E. Thomas 1904 (league record)

Strikeouts 325 Harry Ables 1910 (league record)

Strikeouts in a Game 20 Willie Mitchell Aug. 21,1909 (Bob Turley struckout 22 vs Tulsa Aug. 11,1951 in 16-inning game ending in 3-3 tie).

ERA 1.20 John Whitehead 1 942

Shutouts 7 Maury Newlin 1940

Saves 36 Jared Hoerman 2003

Winning Percentage .824 (14-3) Dennis Eckersley 1974

Most Consecutive Wins 10 Charlie Weber 1897, Bob Muncrief 1940

No-Hitters

Sep. 6,1903 Eddie Taylor vs Galveston Sand Crabs, Mustangs won 3-0 (playoff)

Jun. 22,1905 "Hickory" Clark vs Beaumont Oilers 0-0 tie (11 innings)

Aug. 11,1907 "Buck" Harris at Dallas Giants, Bronchos won 7-1

Jun. 21,1908 Fred Winchell vs Waco Navigators; Winchell held Navs hitless for 11 innings, Waco eventually won 2-0 in 13

Jun. 26,1909 Willie Mitchell vs Shreveport

Pirates, Bronchos won 1-0

Jun. 13,1910 Harry Ables vs Dallas Giants; Ables' no-hitter broken up after 11 innings, San Antonio won 1-0 in 14

Sep. 4,1910 Harry Ables vs Waco Navigators, Bronchos won 1-0 (7 innings)

Jul. 23,1914 George Crabble vs Dallas Giants, Bronchos won 2-1

May 11,1916 Harry Stewart at Waco Navigators, Bronchos won 2-0

Jun. 20,1916 Charlie Harding vs Shreveport Gassers, Bronchos won 2-0

Sep. 7,1919 Barney Burch at Galveston Pirates, Bronchos won 4-0 (7 innings, 2nd game of doubleheader)

Jun. 5,1931 Euel Moore at Galveston Buccaneers, Indians won 3-0

Jul. 31,1940 Loy Hanning vs Tulsa Oilers, Missions won 4-0 (7 innings)

May 14,1944 Bill Haynes vs Dallas Green Monarchs, Black Missions won 1-0

Jun. 24,1951 Tommy Fine at Tulsa Oilers, Missions won 2-0 (7 innings, first game of doubleheader)

Jul. 1,1953 Ryne Duren vs Beaumont Exporters, Missions won 4-1 (7 innings, first game of doubleheader)

May 11,1955 Mel Held vs Fort Worth Cats 0-0 tie (5 innings)

Aug. 31,1955 Don Ferrarese vs Beaumont Exporters, Missions won 3-1 (7 innings, first game of doubleheader)

Jun. 1,1963 Cliff Davis vs El Paso Sun Kings, Bullets won 5-0 (7 innings)

Jun. 5,1968 Dean Burk vs Albuquerque Dodgers, Missions won 1-0 (7 innings, 2nd game of doubleheader)

Jun. 1,1974 Larry Andersen vs Victoria Toros, Brewers won 6-0

May 11,1975 Tom McGough vs Shreveport Captains, Brewers won 1-0

Jul. 4,1979 Rick Goulding at Amarillo Gold Sox, Dodgers won 5-0

Jun. 19,1984 Vance Lovelace, Brian Piper and Steve Martin vs Beaumont Gators, Dodgers won 1-0

Player Representatives in League All-Star Game

1936 Larry Bettencourt, Debs Garms, Sig

Gryska, Art Scharein.
1937 Ollie Bejma, Sig Gryska, Sam
    Harshany, Mel Mazzera, Bob Muncrief,
    Art Scharein.
1938 Sig Gryska, Harry Kimberlin, Ralph
    Rhein, Bill Trotter.
1939 Emil Bildilli, Milt Byrnes, Ed Cole,
    Tony Criscola, Johnny Lucadello, Bob
    Swift.
1940 Jack Bradsher, Sam Harshany, Bob
    Muncrief, Chuck Stevens.
1941 Al White
1948 Bobby Herrera, Tom Jordan, Andy
    Sierra, Bill Sommers.
1949 Tommy Fine, Al Gerheauser, Don
    Lenhardt.
1950 Dan Baich, Frank Biscan, Frank
    Saucier, Lou Sleater, John Sullivan.
1951 Bobby Balcena, Billy Demars, Jim
    Dyck, Babe Martin, Bob Turley.
1952 Bud Black, Charlie Grant, Bud
    Heslet, Babe Martin, Harry Schwegman.
1953 Bobby Balcena, Ryne Duren, Jim
    Fridley, Charlie White, Harry Wilson.
1954 Ryne Duren, Joe Durham, John
    Jancse, Don Masterson.
1955 Mel Held, Charlie Locke, Don
    Masterson, Jim Pisoni.
1956 Carl Scheib
1957 Ron Moeller, Chuck Oertel.
1958 Jim Archer, Carlos Castillo, Harvey
    Cohen, Grady Hatton.
1959 John Goetz, Gordon Massa, Manny
    Montejo.
1960 Jack Curtis, Layton Ducote, Dick
    Getter, Ron Goerger.
1961 Jim Schandevel, Craig Sorensen,
    Morrie Steevens.
1962 Harvey Branch, Don Davis, Don
    Eaddy, Billy Ott, Morrie Steevens.
1963 Cliff Davis, Joe Hoerner, Ed
    Olivares, Mike White.
1964 Don Bradey, Chuck Harrison, Sonny
    Jackson, Joe Morgan, Leo Posada,
    Chris Zachary.
1968 Dave Lemonds
1969 Dean Burk, Brock Davis, John
    Felske, Oscar Gamble.
1970 Adrian Garrett, Pat Jacquez, Jack
    Mull, Don Nottebart, Paul Reuschel.
1971 Billy North

1972 Gorman Thomas, Dennis Yard.
1973 Joe Azcue, Duane Kuiper, Jeff
    Newman, Luis Penalver, Rick Sawyer.
1974 Dennis Eckersley, Jim Strickland.
1975 Gary Weese
1976 Bobby Cuellar, Gary Gray, John Poloni.
1977 Dan Smith, Marv Webb.
1978 Mickey Hatcher, Dave Patterson,
    Kelly Snider, Dave Stewart.
1979 Mark Nipp, Ron Roenicke, Gary Weiss.
1981 Mark Bradley, Dale Holman, Tom
    Niedenfuer, Rich Rodas, Dave Sax,
    Steve Sax, Mike Zouras.
1982 Dab Bilardello, Dean Rennicke,
    Paul Voigt.
1983 Sid Fernandez, Ken Howell, R.J.
    Reynolds.
1984 Ralph Bryant, Gilberto Reyes, Joe Vavra
1985 Jon Debus, Jose Gonzalez, Mark
    Heuer, Scott May, Adrian Meagher.
1986 Mike Devereaux, Chris Gwynn, Ken
    Harvey, Shawn Hillegas, Joe Szekely.
1987 Mike Devereaux, Jack Savage, Joe
    Szekely.
1988 Mike Huff, Luis Lopez, Mike Munoz,
    John Wetteland.
1989 Carlos Hernandez, Dennis Springer.
1990 Kevin Campbell, Mike James, Eric
    Karros, Eddie Pye, Henry Rodriguez,
    Dennis Springer.
1991 Bryan Baar, Tim Barker, Braulio
    Castillo, Eric Young.
1992 Steve Allen, Tim Barker, Matt
    Howard.
1993 Chris Abbe, Rick Gorecki, Todd
    Hollandsworth, Mark Mimbs, Ben Van Ryn.
1994 Chris Demetral, Jay Kirkpatrick,
    Felix Rodriguez.
1995 Miguel Cairo, Gary Rath.
1996 Paul Konerko, Jesus Martinez.
1997 Pat Ahearne, Kevin Gibbs, Joe
    Lagarde, Paul LoDuca, Brian
    Richardson, J.P. Roberge.
1998 Darrin Babineaux, Peter Bergeron,
    Dean Mitchell, Angel Pena, Jon Tucker.
1999 Hiram Bocachica, Eric Gagne, Mike
    Metcalfe, Tony Mota, Matt Montgomery.
2000 Geronimo Gil, Luke Prokopec.
2001 Scott Atchison, Willie Bloomquist,
    Craig Kuzmic, Bo Robinson.
2002 Adrian Myers, Aaron Taylor.

2003 Mike Curry, Travis Blackley, Jim Horner, Rett Johnson, Justin Leone, Jose Lopez, Josue Matos, Clint Nageotte, A.J. Zapp.

Manager Representatives in League All-Star Game

1954 Don Heffner
1955 Don Heffner
1964 Lou Fitzgerald
1973 Tony Pacheco
1980 Don LeJohn
1981 Don LeJohn
1982 Don LeJohn
1988 Kevin Kennedy
1997 Ron Roenicke
2001 Dave Brundage
2003 Dave Brundage

Most Managerial Wins

George Leidy   494-385 .562
Don LeJohn   427-373 .534
Bob Coleman   310-284 .522
Zack Taylor   267-215 .554

Don Heffner   250-226 .525
Hank Severeid   243-221 .524
Gary Larocque   237-304 .438
Dave Brundage   226-190 .543
Grady Hatton   199-191 .510
John Shoemaker   188-218 .463
Jo-Jo White   165-157 .512
Lou Fitzgerald   164-116 .586
Joe Schultz Jr.   152-156 .494
Marty McManus   147-168 .467
Gus Mancuso   145-159 .477
John Nee   139-169 .451
Carl Mitze   134-126 .515
John Shelby   133-142 .484
Walt Dixon   131-149 .468
Ron Roenicke   128-92 .582

Sporting News Minor League Player of the Year

1950 Frank Saucier
1991 Pedro Martinez

Star of Stars Award

1983 Sid Fernandez

Major League Training, Exhibition Games

Spring Training

1904 Cleveland Indians
1906 Cincinnati Reds
1907 St. Louis Browns
1909-10 Detroit Tigers
1912-13 Philadelphia A's
1915 Cleveland Indians
1918 St. Louis Cardinals
1919 St. Louis Browns
1920-23 New York Giants
1921 Detroit Tigers
1924 Boston Red Sox
1926 St. Louis Cardinals
1927-28 Detroit Tigers
1929-31 New York Giants
1930-32 Chicago White Sox
1933 Detroit Tigers
1936 Pittsburgh Pirates
1937-41 St. Louis Browns
1941 Boston Braves
1948 Kansas City Monarchs
1950 Kansas City Monarchs

Exhibition Games

1885
St. Louis Browns

1909
Apr. 22 Leland Giants 5, Black Bronchos 0; Leland Giants 3, Black Bronchos 2

1912
Feb. 28 San Antonio 8 Philadelphia A's 6
Mar. 3 San Antonio 5 Philadelphia A's 4
Mar. 6 San Antonio 7 Philadelphia A's 7
Mar. 9 Philadelphia A's 17 San Antonio 5
Mar. 10 Philadelphia A's 7 San Antonio 6
Mar. 12 San Antonio 10 Philadelphia A's 9
Mar. 13 Philadelphia A's 12 San Antonio 3
Mar. 14 Philadelphia A's 7 San Antonio 3
Mar. 15 Philadelphia A's 5 San Antonio 3
Mar. 16 San Antonio 15 Philadelphia A's 3
Mar. 17 San Antonio 9 Philadelphia A's 7
Mar. 19 Philadelphia A's 10 San Antonio 7
Mar. 20 San Antonio 7 Philadelphia A's 5

Mar. 24 San Antonio 10 Chicago White Sox 6
Mar. 26 Chicago White Sox 12 San Antonio 4
Mar. 27 Chicago White Sox 11 San Antonio 1
Mar. 28 San Antonio 5 Chicago White Sox 0
Mar. 29 Chicago White Sox 8 San Antonio 3

1913
Mar. 1 Philadelphia A's 24 San Antonio 2
Mar. 2 Philadelphia A's 12 San Antonio 5
Mar. 4 Philadelphia A's 14 San Antonio 3
Mar. 6 Philadelphia A's 8 San Antonio 2
Mar. 10 Philadelphia A's 17 San Antonio 1
Mar. 11 Philadelphia A's 3 San Antonio 1
Mar. 15 New York Giants 10 San Antonio 0
Mar. 16 New York Giants 4 San Antonio 2

1914
Mar. 28 New York Giants 1 San Antonio 0
Mar. 29 New York Giants 5 San Antonio 2

1915
Mar. 6 Cleveland Indians 7 San Antonio 4
Mar. 7 Cleveland Indians 4 San Antonio 3
Mar. 13 St. Louis Cardinals 5 Cleveland Indians 1
Mar. 14 St. Louis Cardinals 7 Cleveland Indians 7
Mar. 15 St. Louis Cardinals 12 San Antonio 4
Mar. 16 San Antonio 6 Cleveland Indians 3
Mar. 18 St. Louis Cardinals 18 San Antonio 2
Mar. 20 New York Giants 4 San Antonio 3
Mar. 21 New York Giants 11 San Antonio 0

1916
Mar. 4 San Antonio 6 St. Louis Cardinals 0
Mar. 5 St. Louis Cardinals 11 San Antonio 9
Mar. 11 St. Louis Cardinals 6 San Antonio 4
Mar. 12 San Antonio 7 St. Louis Cardinals 6
Mar. 18 St. Louis Cardinals 8 San Antonio 2
Mar. 19 St. Louis Cardinals 8 San Antonio 2
Mar. 20 New York Giants 13 San Antonio 7
Mar. 21 New York Giants 7 San Antonio 4
Mar. 29 Detroit Tigers 3 San Antonio 0
Mar. 30 Detroit Tigers 5 San Antonio 1
1917
Mar. 10 St. Louis Cardinals 3 San Antonio 1

Mar. 11 St. Louis Cardinals 4 San Antonio 4
Mar. 17 St. Louis Cardinals 7 San Antonio 2
Mar. 18 St. Louis Cardinals 3 San Antonio 3
Mar. 23 St. Louis Browns 1 San Antonio 1
Mar. 24 New York Giants 6 San Antonio 2
Mar. 25 New York Giants 10 San Antonio 0

1918
Mar. 17 San Antonio 4 St. Louis Cardinals 2
Mar. 19 St. Louis Cardinals 19 Kelly Field 2
Mar. 20 St. Louis Cardinals 7 Kelly Field 3
Mar. 23 St. Louis Cardinals 5 San Antonio 4
Mar. 24 St. Louis Cardinals 7 San Antonio 3
Mar. 27 St. Louis Cardinals 3 Camp Travis 0
Mar. 30 New York Giants 8 San Antonio 1
Mar. 31 New York Giants 7 San Antonio 1
Apr. 1 New York Giants 13 Kelly Field 7
Apr. 2 New York Giants 10 Camp Travis 5
Apr. 3 New York Giants 3 San Antonio 1

1919
Mar. 22 St. Louis Browns 6 San Antonio 2
Mar. 23 St. Louis Browns 10 San Antonio 5
Mar. 27 St. Louis Browns 5 Remount No.#2 1
Mar. 29 St. Louis Browns 3 San Antonio 0
Mar. 30 St. Louis Browns 9 San Antonio 5
Apr. 5 St. Louis Browns 9 San Antonio 2
Apr. 6 St. Louis Browns 6 San Antonio 0

1920
Mar. 6 New York Giants 21 San Antonio 1
Mar. 13 New York Giants 12 San Antonio 0
Mar. 14 New York Giants 7 San Antonio 6
Mar. 18 New York Giants 11 San Antonio 1
Mar. 20 St. Louis Browns 9 San Antonio 4
Mar. 21 St. Louis Browns 6 San Antonio 2
Mar. 23 New York Giants 3 San Antonio 1
Mar. 25 Boston Red Sox 3 New York Giants 0
Mar. 31 Chicago White Sox 5 San Antonio 1

1921
Mar. 5 New York Giants 8 San Antonio 3
Mar. 6 New York Giants 15 San Antonio 3
Mar. 12 New York Giants 7 San Antonio 3
Mar. 13 New York Giants 2 San Antonio 0
Mar. 16 New York Giants 6 San Antonio 3
Mar. 19 Detroit Tigers 13 San Antonio 1
Mar. 20 Detroit Tigers 20 San Antonio 0

Mar. 25 Detroit Tigers 19 Camp Travis 1
Mar. 26 Boston Braves 3 San Antonio 2
Mar. 27 Boston Braves 6 San Antonio 1
Mar. 30 Cleveland Indians 9 San Antonio 3
Mar. 31 Cleveland Indians 8 San Antonio 6

1922
Mar. 11 New York Giants 5 Chicago White
Sox 5
Mar. 12 Chicago White Sox 4 New York
Giants 3
Mar. 18 Chicago White Sox 8 New York
Giants 4
Mar. 19 Chicago White Sox 12 New York
Giants 6
Mar. 22 New York Giants 9 Indianapolis
Indians 3
Mar. 23 New York Giants 18 Indianapolis
Indians 7
Mar. 24 New York Giants 4 San Antonio 3
Mar. 25 Philadelphia A's 5 San Antonio 5
Mar. 26 Philadelphia A's 13 San Antonio 0
Mar. 31 New York Yankees 12 Brooklyn
Dodgers 8

1923
Mar. 11 New York Giants 21 San Antonio 14
Mar. 17 Chicago White Sox 6 New York
Giants 4
Mar. 20 New York Giants 21 2nd Engineers
of Ft. Sam Houston 0
Mar. 22 New York Giants 18 San Antonio 5
Mar. 23 Chicago White Sox 5 New York
Giants 3
Mar. 24 Chicago White Sox 9 New York
Giants 9
Mar. 25 New York Giants 8 Chicago
White Sox 6
Mar. 30 New York Giants 5 San Antonio 3
Apr. 5 Chicago Cubs 17 San Antonio 9
Apr. 21 Kansas City Monarchs 12 San
Antonio Black Aces 6

1924
Mar. 9 Boston Red Sox 13 San Antonio 13
Mar. 15 Boston Red Sox 9 San Antonio 3
Mar. 22 Boston Red Sox 13 San Antonio 4
Mar. 23 Boston Red Sox 3 San Antonio 1
Mar. 26 Boston Red Sox 8 San Antonio 6
Mar. 29 Boston Red Sox 5 San Antonio 3
Mar. 30 Boston Red Sox 7 San Antonio 6

1925
Apr. 8 St. Louis Cardinals 15 San Antonio 3

1926
Mar. 6 St. Louis Cardinals 5 San Antonio 1
Mar. 7 St. Louis Cardinals 7 San Antonio 5
Mar. 11 St. Louis Cardinals 12 San Antonio 3
Mar. 12 St. Louis Cardinals 6 San Antonio 3
Mar. 13 St. Louis Cardinals 5 San Antonio 2
Mar. 14 St. Louis Cardinals 8 San Antonio 1
Mar. 21 St. Louis Cardinals 1 San Antonio 0
Mar. 23 St. Louis Cardinals 5 San Antonio 2
Mar. 24 St. Louis Cardinals 3 San Antonio 1
Mar. 27 St. Louis Cardinals 9 San Antonio 6
Mar. 31 San Antonio 3 St. Louis Cardinals 2
Apr. 1 St. Louis Cardinals 6 San Antonio 1

1927
Mar. 12 San Antonio 4 Detroit Tigers 1
Mar. 13 Detroit Tigers 9 San Antonio 4
Mar. 16 Detroit Tigers 7 San Antonio 6
Mar. 17 San Antonio 12 Detroit Tigers 6
Mar. 19 Detroit Tigers 6 San Antonio 4
Mar. 23 Detroit Tigers 8 San Antonio 2
Mar. 24 Detroit Tigers 12 San Antonio 10
Mar. 26 San Antonio 7 Detroit Tigers 2
Mar. 27 Detroit Tigers 6 San Antonio 4
Mar. 30 Detroit Tigers 3 Pittsburgh Pirates 1
Mar. 31 Pittsburgh Pirates 8 Detroit Tigers 4

1928
Mar. 10 Detroit Tigers 8 Minneapolis
Millers 7
Mar. 11 Minneapolis Millers 6 Detroit
Tigers 5
Mar. 15 Detroit Tigers 4 Minneapolis
Millers 2
Mar. 17 Detroit Tigers 1 Minneapolis
Millers 0
Mar. 18 Detroit Tigers 7 Minneapolis
Millers 5
Mar. 23 San Antonio 5 Detroit Tigers 4
Mar. 24 Detroit Tigers 11 San Antonio 5
Mar. 25 Detroit Tigers 9 San Antonio 1
Apr. 4 Pittsburgh Pirates 10 San Antonio 6
Apr. 5 Pittsburgh Pirates 10 San Antonio 1

1929
Mar. 14 New York Giants 15 San Antonio 5
Mar. 16 New York Giants 5 San Antonio 5
Mar. 17 New York Giants 7 San Antonio 1

Mar. 20 New York Giants 7 St. Mary's
   Rattlers 1
Mar. 23 New York Giants 5 Chicago
   White Sox 2
Mar. 24 New York Giants 4 Chicago
   White Sox 3
Mar. 25 New York Giants 11 Kelly Field 2
Mar. 29 New York Giants 6 Pittsburgh
   Pirates 3
Mar. 30 Pittsburgh Pirates 5 San Antonio 4
Mar. 31 Pittsburgh Pirates 23 San Antonio 9

1930
Mar. 9 New York Giants 6 Chicago White
   Sox 5
Mar. 11 New York Giants 5 Chicago
   White Sox 5
Mar. 12 Chicago White Sox 10 New York
   Giants 6
Mar. 15 New York Giants 6 Chicago
   White Sox 5
Mar. 22 New York Giants 3 Chicago
   White Sox 2
Mar. 23 Chicago White Sox 5 New York
   Giants 1
Mar. 24 New York Giants 3 San Antonio 1
Mar. 25 Chicago White Sox 13 San
   Antonio 12
Mar. 26 New York Giants 9 Chicago
   White Sox 3
Mar. 31 New York Yankees 14 San Antonio 4
Apr. 5 Homestead Grays 10 San Antonio
   Black Indians 8
Apr. 6 San Antonio Black Indians 8
   Homestead Grays 6; Homestead
   Grays 10 San Antonio Black Indians 4
Apr. 7 Homestead Grays 9 San Antonio
   Black Indians 5
May 3 San Antonio Black Indians 4
   Kansas City Monarchs 2

1931
Mar. 14 Chicago White Sox 5 New York
   Giants 2
Mar. 16 New York Giants 9 Chicago
   White Sox 6
Mar. 23 New York Giants 6 Chicago
   White Sox 2
Mar. 24 New York Giants 7 San Antonio 3
Mar. 25 New York Giants 17 Chicago
   White Sox 8
Mar. 26 San Antonio 12 Chicago White

   Sox 10
Mar. 28 Chicago White Sox 2 New York
   Giants 1
Mar. 29 New York Giants 15 Chicago
   White Sox 7
Apr. 1 San Antonio 12 New York Giants 6
Apr. 4 New York Giants 6 San Antonio 2
Apr. 5 San Antonio 3 New York Giants 2
October 17 Kansas City Monarchs vs
   Mexico Nationals
October 18 Kansas City Monarchs vs
   Mexico Nationals
October 19 Kansas City Monarchs vs
   Texas League All-Stars
October 20 Kansas City Monarchs vs
   Texas League All-Stars

1932
Mar. 19 Chicago White Sox 16 San Antonio 2
Mar. 20 Chicago White Sox 7 San Antonio 4
Mar. 23 Chicago White Sox 13 San Antonio 5
Aug. 20 Monroe Monarchs vs Austin
   Black Senators

1934
Apr. 4 Chicago Cubs 24 San Antonio 21
Apr. 5 Chicago Cubs 13 San Antonio 0

1936
Mar. 17 Chicago Cubs 3 Pittsburgh Pirates 1
Mar. 18 Chicago Cubs 4 Pittsburgh Pirates 0
Mar. 21 Pittsburgh Pirates 18 San Antonio 4
Mar. 22 Pittsburgh Pirates 11 San Antonio 4
Mar. 25 Pittsburgh Pirates 21 San Antonio 2
Mar. 28 Pittsburgh Pirates 4 Chicago
   White Sox 3
Mar. 29 Pittsburgh Pirates 10 Chicago
   White Sox 8
Apr. 6 St. Louis Cardinals 9 San Antonio 2

1937
Mar. 21 Minneapolis Millers 8 St. Louis
   Browns 4
Mar. 28 Minneapolis Millers 6 St. Louis
   Browns 1
Apr. 2 St. Louis Browns 8 Philadelphia A's 6
Apr. 3 Philadelphia A's 10 St. Louis Browns 0
Apr. 4 Philadelphia A's 4 St. Louis Browns 1
Apr. 5 Kansas City Blues 8 St. Louis
   Browns 6
Apr. 6 St. Louis Browns 11 Kansas City
   Blues 3

Apr. 8 St. Louis Browns 4 Chicago Cubs 3
Apr. 9 Chicago Cubs 8 St. Louis Browns 1
Apr. 10 Chicago Cubs 10 St. Louis
    Browns 6
Apr. 11 Chicago Cubs 9 St. Louis Browns 5

1938
Mar. 18 St. Louis Browns 18 Tulsa Oilers 3
Mar. 19 St. Louis Browns 4 Tulsa Oilers 3
Mar. 20 St. Louis Browns 9 Tulsa Oilers 4
Mar. 31 St. Louis Browns 7 Toledo
    Mudhens 6
Apr. 1 St. Louis Browns 11 Toledo
    Mudhens 2
Apr. 2 St. Louis Browns 3 Toledo Mudhens 0
Apr. 3 St. Louis Browns 8 Toledo Mudhens 3
Apr. 4 St. Louis Browns 4 Toledo Mudhens 3
Apr. 9 Chicago Cubs 5 St. Louis
    Browns 2
Apr. 10 St. Louis Browns 7 Chicago Cubs
    5; St. Louis Browns 5 Chicago Cubs 4

1939
Mar. 12 St. Louis Browns 11 Philadelphia
    Phillies 6
Mar. 15 St. Louis Browns 11 Philadelphia
    Phillies 10
Mar. 18 St. Louis Browns 3 Philadelphia
    Phillies 1
Mar. 19 St. Louis Browns 2 Philadelphia
    Phillies 1
Mar. 31 Philadelphia Phillies 4 St. Louis
    Browns 0
Apr. 3 New York Yankees 9 San Antonio 2
Apr. 4 Pittsburgh Pirates 14 St. Louis
    Browns 1
Apr. 5 Pittsburgh Pirates 7 St. Louis Browns 4
Apr. 8 St. Louis Browns 11 Chicago Cubs 10
Apr. 9 Chicago Cubs 13 St. Louis Browns 4

1940
Mar. 16 Tulsa Oilers 9 St. Louis Browns 7
Mar. 17 St. Louis Browns 12 Tulsa Oilers 4
Mar. 19 St. Louis Browns 6 Toledo
    Mudhens 4
Mar. 20 St. Louis Browns 14 Tulsa Oilers 0
Mar. 21 St. Louis Browns 9 Toledo Mudhens 2
Mar. 22 St. Louis Browns 12 Tulsa Oilers 3
Mar. 23 St. Louis Browns 10 Tulsa Oilers 2
Mar. 24 St. Louis Browns 4 Toledo
    Mudhens 3

Mar. 30 St. Louis Browns 6 Toledo
    Mudhens 5; Tulsa Oilers 7 St. Louis
    Browns 0
Mar. 31 St. Louis Browns 9 Toledo
    Mudhens 5
Apr. 1 New York Yankees 9 San Antonio 3
Apr. 6 Chicago Cubs 7 St. Louis Browns 2
Apr. 28 Indianapolis Crawfords 3
    Mexican All-Stars 0
Jul. 16 Indianapolis Crawfords vs
    Mexican All-Stars

1941
Mar. 8 St. Louis Browns 9 Boston Braves 5
Mar. 9 Boston Braves 11 St. Louis
    Browns 5
Mar. 11 Boston Braves 8 Randolph Field
    Ramblers 0
Mar. 12 St. Louis Browns 9 Boston
    Braves 1
Mar. 21 St. Louis Browns 8 Randolph
    Field Ramblers 4; St. Louis Browns 5
    Minneapolis Millers 0
Mar. 22 Boston Braves 3 St. Louis Browns 2
Mar. 23 Boston Braves 5 St. Louis Browns 4
Mar. 27 Boston Braves 7 Minneapolis
    Millers 6
Mar. 28 Minneapolis Millers 5 Boston
    Braves 3
Mar. 29 Boston Braves 7 St. Louis Browns 4
Mar. 30 St. Louis Browns 18 Boston
    Braves 2
Mar. 31 New York Yankees 16 San Antonio 4

1944
Apr. 19 Kansas City Monarchs vs
    Cincinnati Clowns
Apr. 28 New York Cubans 5 Kansas City
    Monarchs 2
Apr. 29 New York Cubans 7 Kansas City
    Monarchs 4
May 10 Kansas City Monarchs vs
    Memphis Red Sox
Sep. 19 Kansas City Monarchs vs
    Cincinnati Clowns
Sep. 20 Kansas City Monarchs vs
    Cincinnati Clowns
Oct. 8 New York Cubans 6 Charlie Engle
    Army All-Stars 5
October 9 New York Cubans 10 Charlie
    Engle Army All-Stars 4

1945

Apr. 1 Kansas City Monarchs 4 Charlie Engle All-Stars 4

Apr. 12 Chicago American Giants vs Lonnie Greer All-Stars

Apr. 13 Chicago American Giants vs Lonnie Greer All-Stars

Apr. 17 Cleveland Buckeyes 6 Chicago American Giants 5

Apr. 18 Cleveland Buckeyes 10 Chicago American Giants 7

Apr. 26 Homestead Grays vs Lonnie Greer All-Stars

Apr. 27 Homestead Grays vs Lonnie Greer All-Stars

Apr. 27 Kansas City Monarchs vs Indianapolis Clowns

Apr. 28 Kansas City Monarchs vs Indianpolis Clowns

1946

Apr. 2 Chicago White Sox 3 Pittsburgh Pirates 1

Apr. 3 Chicago White Sox 6 Pittsburgh Pirates 2

Apr. 4 St. Louis Browns 10 Chicago Cubs 7

Apr. 5 St. Louis Browns 1 Chicago Cubs 0

Apr. 24 Kansas City Monarchs 6 Chicago American Giants 5

1947

Sep. 28 Kansas City Monarchs vs Indianapolis Clowns

1948

Apr. 3 St. Louis Browns 9 Chicago Cubs 6

Apr. 4 St. Louis Browns 2 Chicago Cubs 1

Apr. 5 St. Louis Browns 8 Chicago Cubs 3

Apr. 8 Pittsburgh Pirates 7 Chicago White Sox 4

Apr. 9 Chicago White Sox 4 Pittsburgh Pirates 3; Kansas City Monarchs vs Black All-Stars

Apr. 10 Pittsburgh Pirates 12 Chicago White Sox 4

Apr. 11 Chicago White Sox 5 Pittsburgh Pirates 1

May 12 Kansas City Monarchs vs Harlem Globetrotters baseball team

May 14 Kansas City Monarchs vs Harlem Globetrotters baseball team

1949

Mar. 31 Brooklyn Dodgers 8 San Antonio 1

Apr. 2 Chicago Cubs 5 St. Louis Browns 4

Apr. 3 Chicago Cubs 3 St. Louis Browns 1

Apr. 5 Chicago White Sox 7 Pittsburgh Pirates 6

Apr. 6 Chicago White Sox 7 Pittsburgh Pirates 1

Apr. 24 Kansas City Monarchs vs Indianapolis Clowns

May 16 Kansas City Monarchs vs Houston Eagles

May 17 Kansas City Monarchs vs Houston Eagles

Jul. 11 Indianapolis Clowns vs Houston Eagles

Aug. 2 Industriales de Monterrey 6 Houston Eagles 2

Sep. 4 Industriales de Monterrey 10 Houston Eagles 6

Sep. 5 Industriales de Monterrey 9 Houston Eagles 3

Sep. 19 Houston Eagles vs New Orleans Creoles

Sep. 25 Indianapolis Clowns 11 Kansas City Monarchs 8

Sep. 26 Kansas City Monarchs 5 Indianapolis Clowns 1

1950

Apr. 1 St. Louis Browns 9 Chicago White Sox 3

Apr. 2 Chicago White Sox 6 St. Louis Browns 0

Apr. 3 Chicago White Sox 9 St. Louis Browns 5

Apr. 4 Cleveland Indians 7 New York Giants 6

Apr. 6 St. Louis Browns 14 Chicago Cubs 2

Apr. 7 St. Louis Browns 11 San Antonio 3

Apr. 8 St. Louis Browns 7 San Antonio 0

Apr. 9 St. Louis Browns 8 San Antonio 2; Kansas City Monarchs 13 San Antonio Aztecs 0

1951

Mar. 31 Chicago White Sox 7 St. Louis Browns 5

Apr. 1 Chicago White Sox 8 St. Louis Browns 7

Apr. 5 New York Yankees 13 San Antonio 10; St. Louis Browns 14 BAMC Comets 9

Apr. 7 St. Louis Browns 5 San Antonio 2
Apr. 8 St. Louis Browns 11 San Antonio 5

1952
Mar. 30 Pittsburgh Pirates 6 St. Louis
Browns 4
Apr. 1 Chicago Cubs 4 Chicago White Sox 2
Apr. 2 Chicago Cubs 3 BAMC Comets 1
Apr. 3 Chicago White Sox 2 St. Louis
Browns 1
Apr. 4 St. Louis Browns 5 Chicago White
Sox 4
Apr. 5 St. Louis Browns 7 BAMC Comets
3; St. Louis Browns 7 San Antonio 3
Apr. 6 St. Louis Browns 18 San Antonio 5
Apr. 7 Cleveland Indians 8 New York
Giants 3
Apr. 14 Kansas City Monarchs 3
Memphis Red Sox 1

1953
Mar. 31 Chicago White Sox 14 BAMC
Comets 4
Apr. 3 St. Louis Browns 5 Chicago Cubs 3
Apr. 4 St. Louis Browns 3 BAMC Comets
2; Chicago Cubs 7 St. Louis Browns 5
Apr. 5 Chicago Cubs 9 St. Louis Browns
8; St. Louis Browns 5 San Antonio 5

1954
Apr. 5 Chicago White Sox 6 St. Louis
Cardinals 2
1955
Mar. 31 Cleveland Indians 14 New York
Giants 11
Apr. 2 Chicago Cubs 16 San Antonio 10
Apr. 3 Chicago Cubs 12 San Antonio 3

1956
Apr. 6 Chicago Cubs 15 Baltimore
Orioles 11
Apr. 7 Pittsburgh Pirates 9 Kansas City A's 2
Apr. 8 Kansas City A's 4 Pittsburgh Pirates 0

1957
Apr. 4 Brooklyn Dodgers 14 Milwaukee
Braves 8
Apr. 5 Chicago Cubs 6 Baltimore Orioles 4
Apr. 6 Baltimore Orioles 10 Chicago Cubs 3

Apr. 7 Chicago Cubs 8 Baltimore Orioles 6

1958
Apr. 6 San Francisco Giants 9 Cleveland
Indians 7

1961
Apr. 6 Chicago Cubs 9 Boston Red Sox 5
May 27 Indianapolis Clowns vs New York
Royals
May 28 Indianapolis Clowns vs New York
Royals

1962
Apr. 5 Houston Colt 45s 3 Los Angeles
Angels 2
Apr. 7 Los Angeles Angels 2 Houston
Colt 45s 1
Apr. 8 Houston Colt 45s 8 Los Angeles
Angels 4

1963
Aug. 1 Texas League All-Stars 7 Houston
Colt 45s 3

1964
Apr. 14 Houston Colt 45s 10 San Antonio 2
Aug. 20 Texas League All-Stars 8
Houston Colt 45s 7

1968
Apr. 4 Chicago Cubs 11 Chicago White
Sox 6

1973
Apr. 4 Cleveland Indians 4 Texas Rangers 3
Apr. 5 Cleveland Indians 4 Texas Rangers 0

1976
Aug. 2 Texas Rangers 18 Texas League
All-Stars 4

1978
Apr. 3 Houston Astros 8 Texas Rangers 3

1999
Apr. 3 Houston Astros 8 Detroit Tigers 3

2001
May 24 San Antonio 14 Seattle Mariners 2

8. Football Facts and Figures

Teams

1967

Toros

Texas Football League champions

Record: 14-0

Head Coach: Duncan McCauley

League: Texas Football League

Stadium: Northeast Stadium, Edgewood Stadium

Owner: Alton Fairchild

Pres./GM: Alton Fairchild

Attendance: 53,600

Playoffs: League championship Dec. 2 at San Antonio 27 Tulsa Thunderbirds 7

Roster:

Alfredo Avila	Stu McBirnie
James Brown	Clarence Miles
Tom Bedick	Gayland Miles
Fred Edwards	Terry Oglesby
Rey Farias	Luz Pedraza
Bill Farrar	David Pullin
Harold Fisher	Ronnie Riddle
Truman Franks	Laszlo Simon
Ken Ferguson	Jerry Smith
George Gaiser	Louis Spreen
Roger Gill	Jim Stewart
Lynn Hooper	Dave Walston
Ken Hudson	Ural White
Bill Lehman	Jerry Williamson
A. C. Lex	Isador Hannah

1968

Toros

Texas Football League champions

Record: 11-1

Head Coach: Duncan McCauley out Sep. 16 (4-0), Hoover Evans in Sep. 17 (7-1)

League: Texas Football League

Stadium: Alamo Stadium

Owner: Alton Fairchild

President/General Manager: P.J. Beurlot

Attendance: 30,518

Playoffs: League championship, Dec. 7 at San Antonio 21 Texarkana Titans 16

Roster:

Marc Allen	Bill Grindle
Andy Anderson	Roy Hitchings
Alfredo Avila	Ken Hudson
Tom Bedick	Keith Hunt
James Brown	Bill Lehman
Lemuel Cook	Joe Lewallen
Mike Dworaczyk	A. C. Lex
Fred Edwards	Johnny Mata
Rey Farias	Clarence Miles
Bill Farrar	Gayland Miles
Gus Fincke	Luz Pedraza
Truman Franks	Louis Spreen
Fred Frieling	Jim Stewart
RogerGill	J. V. Stokes
Frank Goodish	Joe Bednarski
Sonny Detmer	Fred Ekmak
John Erskine	Les Lindsay
Stu McBirnie	Stanley Randle
Billy Bob Stewart	Bob Wade
Dave Walston	

1969

Toros

Texas Football League champions

Record: 7-4

Head Coach: Hoover Evans

League: Continental Football League

Stadium: Harlandale Memorial Stadium, Alamo Stadium

Owner: Henry Hight

President/General Manager: Henry Hight

Attendance: 42,731

Playoffs: Division championship, Nov. 29 San Antonio 20 at Texarkana Titans 7; semifinals Dec. 7 at San Antonio 21 Las Vegas Cowboys 17; league championship Dec. 13 at Indianapolis 44 San Antonio 38 OT

Roster:

Marc Allen	Bill Lehman
Alfredo Avila	Joe Lewallen
Tom Bedick	A. C. Lex
James Brown	Lee Lindsay

Lemuel Cook   Obert Logan
Mike Dworaczyk   Johnny Mata
Ronnie Ehrig   Clarence Miles
Buddy Eiler   Jerry Moritz
Truman Franks   David Morrison
Fred Frieling   Sal Olivas
Roger Gill   Jerry Oliver
Rocky Goodman   Leo Seitz
Bill Grindle   Louis Spreen
William Hines   J. V. Stokes
John Holland   Ruben Whitney
Sonny Detmer   Les Obie

1970
Toros
Texas Football League champions
Record: 8-2
Head Coach: George Pasterchick
League: Texas Football League
Stadium: Harlandale Memorial Stadium
Owner: Henry Hight
President/General Manager: Henry Hight
Attendance: 26,414
Playoffs: at San Antonio vs Omaha
    Mustangs; financially strapped Omaha
    could not make the trip to San Antonio;
    league championship Nov. 21 at San
    Antonio 21 Fort Worth Braves 17
Roster:
Alfredo Avila   Bob Magee
James Brown   Johnny Mata
Mike Carroll   Pat McGill
Lemuel Cook   Clarence Miles
Truman Franks   Sal Olivas
Roger Gill   Jerry Oliver
William Hines   Luz Pedraza
John Holland   J. V. Stokes
Walter Jefferson   Mickel Tiner
R.A. Johnson   Curley Watters
Bill Lehman   Ruben Whitney
A.C. Lex   Joe Womack

Eagles
Record: 12-4
Head Coach: Jerry Wilton
League: United Independent Football League
Owner: Jerry Wilton

1971
Toros
Texas Football League Champions

Record: 4-1
Head Coach: George Pasterchick
League: Trans-American League
Stadium: North East Stadium
Owner: Henry Hight
President/General Manager: Henry Hight
Attendance: 12,248
Playoffs: League championship Jun. 19 at
    San Antonio 20 Texarkana Titans 19
Roster:
Marc Allen   Bill Lehman
Alfredo Avila   Joe Lewallen
Jerry Bettis   Bob Magee
James Brown   Johnny Mata
Lemuel Cook   Pat McGill
Ronnie Ehrig   Clarence Miles
Buddy Eilers   Sal Olivas
Truman Franks   Jerry Oliver
Bill Grindle   Louis Spreen
Isadore Hannah   Skippy Spruill
William Hines   J. V. Stokes
John Holland   Bobby Wade
Keith Hunt   Curley Watters
R.A. Johnson   Ruben Whitney

Eagles
Record: 19-1
Head Coach: Jerry Wilton
League: United Independent Football
    League

1972
Toros
**Southwestern Football League
    Champions**
Record: 8-0
Head Coach: George Pasterchick
League: Southwestern Football League
Stadium: Northside Stadium
Owner: Henry Hight
President/General Manager: Henry Hight
Attendance: 50,650; season ended pre-
    maturely with two games left due to
    financial problems.
Roster:
Marc Allen   Sam Holden
Alfredo Avila   John Holland
Jerry Bettis   Keith Hunt
Don Burrell   Clarence Jackson
Mike Carroll   Joe Lewallen
Lemuel Cook   Johnny Mata

Ken Cooper
Earl Costley
Willie Crafts
Charlie Duke
Jim Duncan
Buddy Eilers
George Gaiser
Roger Gill
Dave Green
Bill Grindle
Tommy Head
William Hines

Shawn Meagher
Clarence Miles
Mike Montgomery
David Munden
Bill Nunnallee
Sal Olivas
Jerry Oliver
Luz Pedraza
Macon Roemer
J. V. Stokes
Curley Watters

Eagles
**United Independent Football League
champions**
Record: 17-2
Head Coach :Jerry Wilton
League: United Independent Football
League
Playoffs: League championship, Dec. 3
San Antonio Eagles defeated Dallas
Panthers

1973
Toros
Record: 6-2
Head Coach: George Pasterchick
League: Southwestern Football League
Stadium: Northside Stadium, Alamo
Stadium
Owner: Henry Hight
President/General Manager: Henry Hight
Attendance: 52,051
Playoffs: semifinals Sep. 1 at San Antonio
45 Las Vegas Casinos 3; league
championship Sep. 9 Oklahoma City
Wranglers 19 at San Antonio 16
Roster:
Marc Allen
Alfredo Avila
Bruce Bealor
Don Burrell
Mike Carroll
Lemuel Cook
Ken Cooper
Buddy Eilers
George Gaiser
Roger Gill
Bill Grindle
Sherill Grubbs

Bill Keresztry
Steve Laidlaw
Bob Magee
Johnny Mata
Shawn Meagher
Clarence Miles
Mike Montgomery
David Munden
Bill Nunnallee
Jerry Oliver
Luz Pedraza
Andrew Perry

William Hines
John Holland
Keith Hunt
Royce Johnson
Jim Duncan

Macon Roemer
Steve Sanders
J. V. Stokes
Curley Watters
Jeff Herman

Eagles
**United Independent Football League
champions**
Record: 12-0
Head Coach: Jerry Wilton
League: United Independent Football League

1974
Toros
Mid-America League co-champions with
Oklahoma City
Record: 5-2
Head Coach: George Pasterchick
League: Mid-America League
Stadium: Northside Stadium
Owner: Henry Hight
President/General Manager: Henry Hight
Attendance: 15,651
Roster:
Willie Adams
Alfredo Avila
Lemuel Cook
Ken Cooper
Royce Johnson
Buddy Eilers
Bill Grindle
Sherill Grubbs
Phil Hahan
John Holland
Johnny Mata

Al Mays
Clarence Miles
David Munden
Joe Nedros
Bill Nunnallee
Luz Pedraza
Leo Seitz
J. V. Stokes
Curley Watters
Bennie Wilson
David Yaege

Eagles
Record: 6-3-1
Head Coach: Jerry Wilton
League: United Independent Football League

1975
Wings
Record: 7-6
Head Coach: Perry Moss
League: World Football League
Stadium: Alamo Stadium
President/General Manager: Norm Bevan
Attendance: 93,497
Roster:
Chuck Beatty
Bill Kerecsztury

Bruce Bealor
Tim Brannan
Butch Brezina
Rick Cash
Richard Cheek
Steve Conley
Jay Corey
Larry Crowe
Jerry Davis
Nate Dorsey
Jim Ettinger
Willie Frazier
Billy Hayes
Emery Hicks
Billy Hobbs
Tom Hoffman
Hugo Hollas
Larry Jameson
Sherman Jarmon
Tom Johnson
Mark Kellar

Joe Lewallen
Billy Line
Chris Morris
Donnie Joe Morris
Luther Palmer
Hal Phillips
Eddie Richardson
Ernie Richardson
Bill Sadler
J. V. Stokes
Jim Strong
Willie Tolbert
Gary Valbuena
Paul Vellano
Johnny Walton
Lonnie Warwick
Everett Williams
Craig Wiseman
Joe Womack
David Yaege

Eagles
Head Coach: Jerry Wilton
League: United Independent Football League

1976
Toros
Record: 2-0
Head Coach: George Pasterchick
League: Mid-America League
Stadium: Northside Stadium
Owner: Henry Hight
President/General Manager: Henry Hight
Attendance: 7,913; rest of season cancelled
Roster:

Willie Adams
Alfredo Avila
Bruce Bealor
Earl Costley
Buddy Eilers
Jim Ettinger
Mike Garner
Roger Gill
Chuck Gossett
John Holland
James Johnson
Dudley Kellar
Bill Keresztury
Greg Lenz

Bob Magee
Al Mays
Ken Mills
Johnny Moore
David Munden
Leon O'Neal
Jim Roberts
Clay Roland
Steve Sanders
Pat Scully
George Short
Gary Shuler
J.V. Stokes
David Yaege

Eagles
League: United Independent Football League
GM: Marvin Sawyer

1977
Charros
**American Football Association
champions**
Record: 8-0
Head Coach: Harry Lander
League: American Football Association
Stadium: Harlandale Memorial Stadium,
    South San Stadium, Alamo Stadium,
    Northside Stadium.
Owner: Harry Lander
President/General Manager: Harry Lander
Attendance: 7,700
Roster:

Clarence Alberts
Alfredo Avila
Bob Dunn
Chuck Gossett
Joe Gross
Grady Hoermann
Allen Kaier
Dudley Keller
Rich Lander
Greg Lens
Bob Magee
David McLeod
Ken Mills
Mike Morrison
David Munden

Glen Penna
Fred Pointer
Robert Rickman
D. W. Rutledge
Bobby Sagebiell
Gary Shuler
John Sloan
Joe Stair
Howard Stearns
J. V. Stokes
David Wehmeyer
Mike Wendell
Rhiny Williams
Ricky Williams

1978
Charros
Record: 6-4
Head Coach: George Pasterchick
League: American Football Association
Stadium: Harlandale Memorial Stadium
Owner: Roger Gill
President/General Manager: Roger Gill
Attendance: 9,000
Playoffs: Aug. 26 at San Antonio 25
    Houston Titans 7; division champion-
    ship Sep. 16 at Shreveport Steamer 17
    San Antonio 14
Roster:

Clarence Alberts
Alfredo Avila
Darrell Danklefs

Raul Reynosa
J. V. Stokes
Carl Tolbert

Scott DeShay	Buddy Tomasi
Joe Gross	John Tuttle
Jonathan Hooks	Robert Valdez
Roy Hubbard	Pat Walker
Dudley Keller	David Wehmeyer
John Martinez	Tom Whittier
Ken Mills	Rhiny Williams
Millard Neely	Ricky Williams
Fred Pointer	

Eagles
League: United Independent Football League

Apaches
League: United Independent Football League

1979
Charros
Record: 10-4
Head Coach: George Pasterchick
League: American Football Association
Stadium: Alamo Stadium
Owner: Roger Gill
President/General Manager: Roger Gill
Attendance: 32,500
Playoffs: semifinals Sep. 16 at Carolina Chargers 28 San Antonio 21
Roster:

Tony Armstrong	David Munden
Leonard Brantley	Millard Neely
Willie Burleson	Keith Nelms
Steve Carroll	Frank Oakes
Darrell Danklefs	Luz Pedraza
Bruce Dickey	Fred Pointer
Tommy Duniven	Robert Rickman
Clyde Jenkins	Howard Stearns
Randy Johnson	J. V. Stokes
Allen Kaiser	Buddy Tomasi
Glen Kaiser	Pat Walker
Dudley Keller	Mike Washington
Bucky Lampe	David Wehmeyer
Johnny Martinez	Thomas Whittier
Mike McLeod	Ricky Williams

1980
Charros
Record: 6-4
Head Coach: George Pasterchick
League: American Football Association
Stadium: Alamo Stadium, Harlandale Memorial Stadium

Owner: Roger Gill
President/General Manager: Roger Gill
Attendance: 10,827
Playoffs: semifinals Aug. 30 at Carolina Chargers 36 San Antonio 20
Roster:

Willie Adams	Keith Nelms
Ken Daley	Anton Niles
Dave Devire	Frank Oakes
Steve Ferrell	Carlos Perez
Phil Hahn	Fred Pointer
Steve Holson	Robert Rickman
Clyde Jenkins	James Roberts
Randy Johnson	Mike Thierry
Dudley Keller	Buddy Tomasi
Bucky Lampe	Bruce Trimmier
John Martinez	John Tuttle
Ken Mills	Robert Valdez
Tom Nance	Thomas Whittier
Tally Neal	Ricky Williams

1981
Charros
Record: 6-6
Head Coach: George Pasterchick
League: American Football Association
Stadium: Harlandale Memorial Stadium
Owner: Roger Gill
President/General Manager: Roger Gill
Attendance: 18,000
Playoffs: Aug. 23 at Charleston Rockets 41 San Antonio 12
Roster:

Willie Adams	John Martinez
Clarence Alberts	Mike McLeod
Mark Allen	Ken Mills
Tim Bailey	Robert Moszee
Bruce Bealor	Keith Nelms
Steve Breed	Anton Niles
Mark Cahill	Frank Oakes
Sonny Calvert	Steve Pasterchick
T.J. Crawford	Glenn Penna
Darrell Danklefs	Carlos Perez
Reginald Deloney	James Roberts
Bon Dunn	Joe Rodriguez
Steve Ferrell	Ed Rowley
Pete Gibbons	Chester Scroggins
Benny Goodwin	Jerome Sellers
Casterdale Green	Clarence Stewart
Phil Hahn	Mike Thiery
Clyde Jenkins	Buddy Tomasi

Dudley Keller
Bill Keresctury
Joe Keresctury
Bucky Lampe
Rich Lander
Al Lee
Kevin Linam
Jimmy MacPatton

Charlie Trotman
Joe Tucker
Robert Valdez
David Wehmeyer
Calvin Williams
Carl Williams
Len Williams
Jim Young

1982
Bulls
Record: 4-6
Head Coach: George Pasterchick
League: American Football Association
Stadium: Northside Stadium, Harlandale
  Memorial Stadium, Alamo Stadium
Owner: Clinton Manges
President: Pat Maloney
General Manager: Roger Gill
Attendance: 44,200

1983
Bulls
Record: 6-1
Head Coach: Roger Gill
League: American Football Association
Stadium: Harlandale Memorial Stadium
Attendance: 8,406
Playoffs: League championship
July 23 at Carolina Storm 39 San Antonio 0

1984
Gunslingers
Record: 7-11
Head Coach: Gil Steinke
League: United States Football League
Stadium: Alamo Stadium
Owner: Clinton Manges
President: M. W. " Bud"□ Haun
General Manager: Roger Gill
Attendance: 138,996
Roster:

Greg Anderson
Tony Armstrong
John Barefield
Vance Bedford
Marcus Bonner
Danny Buggs
Frank Case
Juan Castillo
Putt Choate

Rick Neuheisel
Reggie Oliver
Larry O'Roark
Richard Osborne
Rodney Parker
Jim Pekar
Lonell Phea
Ernest Price
David Pryor

Rich D'Amico
Greg Davidson
Karl Douglas
Mike Ford
Rich Garza
Ken Gillen
Joey Hackett
Mike Hagen
Paul Hanna
Larry James
Gary Don Johnson
Ron Kirkpatrick
Glenn McCormick
Nick Mike-Mayer
Terry Monroe
Jim Bob Morris
Daryl Mueske
Tally Neal
Keith Nelms

Peter Raeford
Rock Richmond
Don Roberts
Joe Silipo
Lee Spivey
Scott Stamper
Mike St. Clair
Glenn Starks
Tommy Tabor
Arland Thompson
Maurice Tyler
Mike Ulmer
Raymond Waddy
Al Penn-White
Jafus White
Victor White
Ralph Williams
Jon Zogg

1985
Gunslingers
Record: 5-13
Head Coach: Jim Bates out May 18 (3-9),
  Gil Steinke in May 19 (2-4)
League: United States Football League
Stadium: Alamo Stadium
Owner: Clinton Manges
President: M.W. "Bud"□ Haun
General Manager: Roger Gill
Attendance: 103,989
Roster:

Brad Anae
Charles Armstead
John Barefield
Marcus Bonner
Danny Buggs
Larry Canada
Jeff Chaffin
Putt Choate
Rick D'Amico
Greg Fields
Rich Garza
Jeff Gaylord
Ken Gillen
Jerry Gordon
Joey Hackett
James Hadnot
Ken Hartley
Jay Hayes
Al Hill

Nick Mike-Mayer
Vic Minor
Jim Bob Morris
Fred Mortensen
Rick Neuheisel
Reggie Oliver
Peter Raeford
Carl Roberts
Don Roberts
Mark Rosh
Joe Silipo
Bennie Smith
Pete Speros
Lee Spivey
Scott Stamper
Whit Taylor
Arland Thompson
Mark Tolbert
Mike Ulmer

Larry James
Mark Jenkins
Clyde Johnson
Jeff Leiding
Ivan Lesnik
Reggie Mathis

Rod Walters
Leon Williams
Oliver Williams
Ralph Williams
Gary Worthy
Jon Zogg

1991
Riders
Record: 4-6
Head Coach: Mike Riley
League: World League of American
   Football
Stadium: Alamo Stadium
Owner: Larry Benson
General Manager: John Peterson
Attendance: 74,266
Roster:

David Bailey
Stefan Bjorkman
Ricky Blake
Carlos Cheattom
Terrance Cooks
Anthony Cooney
Charlie Darrington
Sean Dykes
John Fletcher
Teddy Garcia
Donnie Gardner
Jason Garrett
John Garrett
Greg Gilbert
Eddie Grant
Broderick Graves
James Harper
Bill Hess
John Husby
J. Hylliermark
Undva Johnson

Mike Kiselak
John Layfield
Mark Ledbetter
Greg Lee
Broderick Manning
Lee Morris
Stefan Ohrvall
Dwight Pickens
Gary Richard
Greg Ross
Marco Rueda
Lee Saltz
Brian Smidler
Kent Sullivan
John Vitale
Ken Walton
Tim Walton
Ken Watson
Ronnie Williams
Kennedy Wilson

1992
Riders
Record: 7-3
Head Coach: Mike Riley
League: World League of American
   Football
Stadium: Bobcat Stadium
Owner: Larry Benson
General Manager: John Peterson
Attendance: 66,538
Roster:

Tony Boles
Ivory Lee Brown
Darrell Colbert
Terrence Cooks
Anthony Cooney
Titus Dixon
Greg Eaglin
Willie Fears
Jim Gallery
Brad Goebel
Eddie Grant
Patrick Hinton
Bobby Humphrey
Malvin Hunter
Mike Johnson
Mike Kiselak
Craig Kupp
Mark Ledbetter
Greg Lee

Ben Mitchell
Lee Morris
Erik Norgard
Chris Oldtham
Gary Richard
Greg Ross
George Searcy
Pete Shorts
Kent Sullivan
Chris Theilman
John Vitale
Wayne Walker
Tim Walton
Danta Whitaker
Robb White
Albert Williams
Doug Williams
Ronnie Williams

Force
Record: 2-8
Head Coach: Dick Nolan
League: Arena Football League
Stadium: HemisFair Arena
Owner: B.J. "Red□" McCombs
General Manager: Dick Nolan
Attendance: 60,077
Roster:

David Caldwell
Thomas Cobb
Keithen DeGrate
Duane Duncum
Smiley Elmore
Anthony Faldyn
Tracy Gordon
James Greene
James Harvey
Alvin Horn
Ken Lutz

Don Maloney
Mike Reneau
Doug Robb
Victor Scott
Scott Segrist
Stephen Shelly
Warren Stewart
Steve Stutsman
Charles Thompson
Dante Williams

1995
Texans
Record: 12-6
Head Coach: Kay Stephenson
League: Canadian Football League
Stadium: Alamodome
Owner: Fred Anderson
General Manager: Kay Stephenson
Attendance: 142,699
Playoffs: Nov. 5 at San Antonio 52

Birmingham Barracudas 9
Division championship game Nov. 12 at
   Baltimore Stallions 21 San Antonio 11
Roster:

Roman Anderson	Bobby Humphery
Dave Archer	Tony Jackson
Brett Bech	Todd Jordan
George Bethune	Jim Kemp
Hurlie Brown	James King
Phil Brown	Mike Kiselak
John Buddenberg	Joe Kralik
Tony Burse	Jimmy Lee
Grady Cavness	Darrin Muilenburg
Andy Cobaugh	Kenny Neal
Roosevelt Collins	Leonard Nelson
Mike Dingle	Mike Saunders
Chuck Esty	Jeff Sawyer
Willie Fears	Peter Shorts
Malcolm Frank	Daryle Smith
David Gamble	Tommie Smith
Joe Garten	Rob Stevenson
Marcus Gates	Mark Stock
Tom Gerhart	Kitrick Taylor
Oscar Giles	Jason Wallace
Dave Harper	Kenny Wilhite
Billy Hess	Myron Wise

1998
Stampede
Record: 8-0
Head Coach: Brian Morgan

League: United States Independent
   Football League

2000
Matadors
Spring Football League co-champions
   with Houston Marshals, decision made
   when league folded
Record: 2-0
Head Coach: Brian Wiggins
League: Spring Football League
Stadium: Alamo Stadium
Owner: Mark Rice
General Manager: Brian Wiggins
Attendance: 3,000

2001
Thunder
Record: 3-7
League: North American Football League
Stadium: Lanier High School, South San
   Antonio Stadium, Alamo Stadium
Owner: Rolf Schaefer
General Manager: Rolf Schaefer

2002
Texas Coyotes (disbanded Jun. 28)
Record: 2-0
League: North American Football League
Stadium: Comalander Stadium
General Manager: Kent Sullivan

Records, Honors, Exhibition Games

League Leaders

Passing: 1975 Johnny Walton Att-338
   Cmp-167 Yds-2405 TD-19
Receptions: 1975 Eddie Richardson No-
   46 Yds-682 Avg-14.8 TD-4
Rushing: 1992 Ivory Lee Brown Car-166
   Yds-767 Avg-4.6 TD-7

All-League Selections

1967 Offense-James Brown RB, George
   Gaiser OT, Roger Gill TE, Luz Pedraza
   QB.
Defense-Alfredo Avila S, Ken Hudson OT,
   Clarence Miles TE.
1969 Offense-James Brown RB, Mike
   Dworaczyk OT, Roger Gill TE, A.C. Lex FB.

Defense-Ronnie Ehrig S, Bill Grindle DE,
   Joe Lewallen DT, Obert Logan S,
   Johnny Mata LB, Clarence Miles DE,
   J.V. Stokes CB.
1972 Offense-Don Burrell SE, Willie
   Crafos G, Roger Gill TE, Tom Head C,
   Bill Nunnallee G, Curley Watters RB.
Defense-Marc Allen, Charlie Duke CB, Bill
   Grindle, William Hines LB, Joe
   Lewallen, J.V. Stokes CB.
1978 First Team Offense-Fred Pointer G,
   John Tuttle WR.
Second Team Offense-John Martinez OT,
   Rich Lander K, David Wehmeyer RB,
   Tom Whittier WR.
First Team Defense-Alfredo Avila DB, Ken
   Mills DT, Millard Neely DT.

Second Team Defense-Bon Dunn LB, Roy Hubbard DE, J.V. Stokes DB, Robert Valdez LB, Rhiny Williams DE, Ricky Williams DB.
1984 Defense-Peter Raeford CB
1991 First Team Offense-Ricky Blake RB
First Team Defense-Tim Walton LB
1992 First Team Offense-Ivory Lee Brown RB, John Vitale C.
First Team Defense-Mark Ledbetter LB, Chris Thieneman DE, Tim Walton LB.
1995 Offense-Roman Anderson K, Mike Kiselak C, Mike Saunders FB.

Coach of the Year
1969 Hoover Evans
1972 George Pasterchick
1972 Jerry Wilton
2000 Brian Wiggins

MVP
1972 Luz Pedraza

Rookie of the Year
1972 Clarence Jackson HB

Most Head Coach Wins
Jerry Wilton 66-10-1 .857 (Incomplete)
George Pasterchick 65-31 .677
Duncan McCauley 18-0 1.000
Hoover Evans 14-5 .737
Kay Stephenson 12-6 .667
Mike Riley 11-9 .550
Gil Steinke 9-15 .375
Harry Lander 8-0 1.000

Perry Moss 7-6 .538
Roger Gill 6-1 .857

Training Camps
1991-96 Houston Oilers
2002-03 Dallas Cowboys

Exhibition Games
1949: Sep. 5 Los Angeles Rams 21 New York Bulldogs 14
1950: Sep. 2 Los Angeles Rams 70 Baltimore Colts 21
1951: Sep. 15 Detroit Lions 21 Chicago Cardinals 7
1952: Sep. 5 Dallas Texans 27 Washington Redskins 14
1953: Sep. 7 San Francisco 49ers 24 Philadelphia Eagles 21
1954: Sep. 17 Philadelphia Eagles 24 Los Angeles Rams 21
1960: Aug. 13 St. Louis Cardinals 20 Dallas Cowboys 13
1965: Aug. 28 Houston Oilers 25 Denver Broncos 3
1968: Aug. 30 San Diego Chargers 6 Denver Broncos 3
1993: Aug. 7 New Orleans Saints 37 Houston Oilers 28; Aug. 21 Houston Oilers 23 Dallas Cowboys 20
1994: Aug. 6 Houston Oilers 31 San Diego Chargers 3; Aug. 20 Buffalo Bills 18 Houston Oilers 16
1995: Aug. 26 Dallas Cowboys 10 Houston Oilers 0
2001: Aug. 11 Minnesota Vikings 28 New Orleans Saints 21

9. Basketball Facts and Figures

Teams

1973–74
Spurs
Record: 45-39
Head Coach: Tom Nissalke
League: American Basketball
  Association
Arena: HemisFair
Chairman: John Schaefer
President: B. J. "Red"☐ McCombs
General Manager: Jack Ankerson
Attendance: 258,434
Playoffs: Indiana 4 San Antonio 3
Roster:

William Averitt	George Karl
Roger Brown	Eugene Kennedy
Jerry Chambers	Swen Nater
Coby Dietrick	Bob Netolicky
George Gervin	James Silas
Joe Hamilton	Harley Swift
Simmie Hill	Chuck Terry
Rich Jones	Bobby Warren

1974–75
Spurs
Record: 51-33
Head Coach: Tom Nissalke out Dec. 13
  (17-10), Bob Bass in Dec. 14 (34-23)
League: American Basketball
  Association
Arena: HemisFair
Chairman: John Schaefer
President: B. J. "Red"☐ McCombs
General Manager: John Begzos
Attendance: 329,844
Playoffs: Indiana 4 San Antonio 2
Roster:

Coby Dietrick	Stan Love
William Franklin	Swen Nater
Donnie Freeman	James Silas
George Gervin	Collis Temple
Rich Jones	Chuck Terry
George Karl	Bobby Warren

1975–76
Spurs
Record: 50-34
Head Coach: Bob Bass
League: American Basketball Association
Arena: HemisFair
President: Angelo Drossos
General Manager: John Begzos
Attendance: 336,083
Playoffs: New York 4 San Antonio 3
Roster:

Allen Bristow	Mark Olberding
Coby Dietrick	Tom Owens
William Franklin	Billy Paultz
Mike Gale	James Silas
George Gervin	Ken Smith
Stew Johnson	Dennis Van Zant
George Karl	Henry Ward
Larry Kenon	Skip Wise

1976–77
Spurs
Record: 44-38
Head Coach: Doug Moe
League: NBA
Arena: HemisFair
President: Angelo Drossos
General Manager: John Begzos
Attendance: 376,136
Playoffs: Boston 2 San Antonio 0
Roster:

Allen Bristow	George Karl
Mack Calvin	Larry Kenon
Louie Dampier	Louie Nelson
Mike D'Antoni	Mark Olberding
Coby Dietrick	Billy Paultz
Mike Gale	James Silas
George Gervin	Henry Ward

1977–78
Spurs
Record: 52-30

Head Coach: Doug Moe
League: NBA
Arena: HemisFair
President: Angelo Drossos
General Manager: John Begzos
Attendance: 373,707
Playoffs: Washington 4 San Antonio 2
Roster:

Allen Bristow	George Karl
Louie Dampier	Larry Kenon
Coby Dietrick	Dennis Layton
Jim Eakins	Mark Olberding
Mike Gale	Billy Paultz
George Gervin	James Silas
Mike Green	Scott Sims

1978–79
Spurs
Record: 48-34
Head Coach: Doug Moe
League: NBA
Arena: HemisFair
President: Angelo Drossos
General Manager: John Begzos
Attendance: 489,207
Playoffs: San Antonio 4 Philadelphia 3
    Washington 4 San Antonio 3
Roster:

Allen Bristow	Larry Kenon
Louie Dampier	Glenn Mosley
Coby Dietrick	Mark Olberding
Mike Gale	Billy Paultz
George Gervin	Frankie Sanders
Mike Green	James Silas

1979–80
Spurs
Record: 41-41
Head Coach: Doug Moe out March 1 (33-33), Bob Bass in March 2 (8-8)
League: NBA
Arena: HemisFair
President: Angelo Drossos
General Manager: Bob Bass
Attendance: 468,657
Playoffs: Houston 2 San Antonio 1
Roster:

Tim Bassett	Sylvester Norris
Harry Davis	Mark Olberding
Mike Evans	Billy Paultz
Mike Gale	Wiley Peck

George Gervin	Kevin Restani
Paul Griffin	John Shumate
Larry Kenon	James Silas
Irv Kiffin	

1980–81
Spurs
Record: 52-30
Head Coach: Stan Albeck
League: NBA
Arena: HemisFair
President: Angelo Drossos
General Manager: Bob Bass
Attendance: 440,553
Playoffs: Houston 4 San Antonio 3
Roster:

Ron Brewer	Reggie Johnson
Dave Corzine	Johnny Moore
Mike Gale	Mark Olberding
Gus Gerard	Kevin Restani
George Gervin	John Shumate
Paul Griffin	James Silas
George Johnson	Michael Wiley

1981–82
Spurs
Record: 48-34
Head Coach: Stan Albeck
League: NBA
Arena: HemisFair
President: Angelo Drossos
General Manager: Bob Bass
Attendance: 434,243
Playoffs: San Antonio 4 Seattle 1
    Los Angeles 4 San Antonio 0
Roster:

Gene Banks	John Lambert
Mike Bratz	Mike Mitchell
Ron Brewer	Johnny Moore
Dave Corzine	Mark Olberding
George Gervin	Roger Phegley
Paul Griffin	Ed Rains
Steve Hayes	Kevin Restani
George Johnson	Rich Yonakor
Reggie Johnson	

1982–83
Spurs
Record: 53-29
Head Coach: Stan Albeck
League: NBA

Arena: HemisFair
President: Angelo Drossos
General Manager: Bob Bass
Attendance: 397,489
Playoffs: San Antonio 4 Denver 1
    Los Angeles 4 San Antonio 2
Roster:

Gene Banks	Mike Mitchell
Geoff Crompton	Johnny Moore
Coby Dietrick	Billy Paultz
Mike Dunleavy	Roger Phegley
George Gervin	Ed Rains
Artis Gilmore	Oliver Robinson
Paul Griffin	Mike Sanders
Jim Johnstone	Robert Smith
Edgar Jones	Bill Willoughby

1983–84
Spurs
Record: 37-45
Head Coach: Morris McHone out Dec. 28
   (11-20), Bob Bass in Dec. 29 (26-25)
League: NBA
Arena: HemisFair
Chairman: Angelo Drossos
General Manager: Bob Bass
Attendance: 375,900
Roster:

Gene Banks	Mark McNamara
Dave Batton	Robert Miller
Ron Brewer	Mike Mitchell
Keith Edmonson	Johnny Moore
George Gervin	John Paxson
Artis Gilmore	Roger Phegley
Edgar Jones	Fred Roberts
Steve Lingenfelter	Dave Robisch
Darrell Lockhart	Brant Weidner
John Lucas	Kevin Williams

1984–85
Spurs
Record: 41-41
Head Coach: Cotton Fitzsimmons
League: NBA
Arena: HemisFair
Chairman: Angelo Drossos
General Manager: Bob Bass
Attendance: 364,398
Playoffs: Denver 3 San Antonio 2
Roster:

Gene Banks	Mark McNamara
Ron Brewer	Mike Mitchell
Jeff Cook	Johnny Moore
George Gervin	John Paxson
Artis Gilmore	Fred Roberts
Marc Iavaroni	Alvin Robertson
Edgar Jones	David Thirdkill
Ozell Jones	Linton Townes
Billy Knight	

1985–86
Spurs
Record: 35-47
Head Coach: Cotton Fitzsimmons
League: NBA
Arena: HemisFair
Chairman: Angelo Drossos
General Manager: Bob Bass
Attendance: 336,407
Playoffs: Los Angeles 3 San Antonio 0
Roster:

Mike Brittain	Jeff Lamp
Jeff Cook	Wes Matthews
Tyrone Corbin	Mike Mitchell
Artis Gilmore	Johnny Moore
David Greenwood	Alvin Robertson
Rod Higgins	Jon Sundvold
Alfredrick Hughes	Ennis Whatley
Marc Iavaroni	Jeff Wilkins
Steve Johnson	Ray Williams

1986–87
Spurs
Record: 28-54
Head Coach: Bob Weiss
League: NBA
Arena: Hemsifair
Chairman: Angelo Drossos
General Manager: Bob Bass
Attendance: 328,368
Roster:

Walter Berry	Larry Krystkowiak
Frank Brickowski	Forrest McKenzie
Mike Brittain	Mike Mitchell
Tyrone Corbin	Johnny Moore
Johnny Dawkins	Ed Nealy
Kevin Duckworth	Alvin Robertson
Artis Gilmore	Jon Sundvold
David Greenwood	Mychal Thompson
Anthony Jones	

1987–88
Spurs
Record: 31-51
Head Coach: Bob Weiss
League: NBA
Arena: HemisFair
Chairman: Angelo Drossos
VP of Basketball Operations: Bob Bass
Attendance: 346,960
Playoffs: Los Angeles 3 San Antonio 0
Roster:

Greg Anderson	Pete Myers
Walter Berry	Ed Nealy
Nate Blackwell	Kurt Nimphius
Frank Brickowski	Richard Rellford
Charles Davis	Alvin Robertson
Johnny Dawkins	Jon Sundvold
David Greenwood	Rick Wilson
Petur Gudmundsson	Leon Wood
Mike Mitchell	Phil Zevenbergen
Johnny Moore	

1988–89
Spurs
Record: 21-61
Head Coach: Larry Brown
League: NBA
Arena: HemisFair
Owner: B. J. "Red" McCombs
VP of Basketball Operations: Bob Bass
Attendance: 459,514
Roster:

Greg Anderson	Albert King
Michael Anderson	Vernon Maxwell
Willie Anderson	Todd Mitchell
Anthony Bowie	Calvin Natt
Frank Brickowski	Alvin Robertson
Dallas Comegys	Scott Roth
Darwin Cook	Keith Smart
Johnny Dawkins	Mike Smrek
David Greenwood	John Stroeder
Petur Gudmundsson	Jay Vincent
Shelton Jones	Jerome Whitehead

1989–90
Spurs
Record: 56-26
Head Coach: Larry Brown
League: NBA
Arena: HemisFair
Owner B. J. "Red" McCombs

VP of Basketball Operations: Bob Bass
Attendance: 603,660
Playoffs: San Antonio 3 Denver 0;
    Portland 4 San Antonio 3
Roster:

Willie Anderson	Vernon Maxwell
Uwe Blab	Johnny Moore
Frank Brickowski	Zarko Paspalj
Maurice Cheeks	David Robinson
Terry Cummings	Rod Strickland
Sean Elliott	Christian Welp
Caldwell Jones	Reggie Williams
Jeff Lebo	David Wingate

1990–91
Spurs
Record: 55-27
Head Coach: Larry Brown
League: NBA
Arena: HemisFair
Chairman: B. J. "Red" McCombs
VP of Basketball Operations: Bob Bass
Attendance: 651,965
Playoffs: Golden State 3 San Antonio 1
Roster:

Willie Anderson	Tony Massenburg
Terry Cummings	Pete Myers
Byron Dinkins	Paul Pressey
Sean Elliott	David Robinson
Sidney Green	Dwayne Schintzius
David Greenwood	Rod Strickland
Sean Higgins	Reggie Williams
Avery Johnson	David Wingate
Clifford Lett	

1991–92
Spurs
Record: 47-35
Head Coach: Larry Brown out Jan. 21
    (21-17), Bob Bass in Jan. 22 (26-18).
League: NBA
Arena: HemisFair
Chairman: B. J. "Red" McCombs
VP of Basketball Operations: Bob Bass
Attendance: 658,337
Playoffs: Phoenix 3 San Antonio 0
Roster:

Willie Anderson	Avery Johnson
Steve Bardo	Vinnie Johnson
Jud Buechler	Tony Massenburg
Antoine Carr	Paul Pressey

Tom Copa
Terry Cummings
Sean Elliott
Tom Garrick
Sidney Green
Sean Higgins

David Robinson
Donald Royal
Rod Strickland
Greg Sutton
Trent Tucker
Morlon Wiley

1992–93
Spurs
Record: 49-33
Head Coach: Jerry Tarkanian out Dec. 18
    (9-11), John Lucas in Dec. 19 (40-22)
League: NBA
Arena: HemisFair
Chairman: B. J. "Red" McCombs
VP of Basketball Operations: Bob Bass
Attendance: 658,337
Playoffs: San Antonio 3 Portland 1
        Phoenix 4 San Antonio 2
Roster:

Willie Anderson
William Bedford
Antoine Carr
Terry Cummings
Lloyd Daniels
Vinny Del Negro
Sean Elliott
Dale Ellis

Sidney Green
Avery Johnson
Sam Mack
Matt Othick
J. R. Reid
David Robinson
Larry Smith
David Wood

1993–94
Spurs
Record: 55-27
Head Coach: John Lucas
League: NBA
Dome: Alamodome
Chairman: Robert McDermott
President: Bob Coleman
VP of Basketball Operations: Bob Bass
Attendance: 904,167
Playoffs: Utah 3 San Antonio 1
Roster:

Willie Anderson
Antoine Carr
Terry Cummings
Lloyd Daniels
Vinny Del Negro
Dale Ellis
Sleepy Floyd

Jack Haley
Negele Knight
Chuck Nevitt
J. R. Reid
David Robinson
Dennis Rodman
Chris Whitney

1994–95
Spurs
Record: 62-20

Head Coach: Bob Hill
League: NBA
Dome: Alamodome
Chairman: Robert McDermott
President: John Diller
General Manager: Gregg Popovich
Attendance: 920,413
Playoffs: San Antonio 3 Denver 0
        San Antonio 4 Los Angeles 2
        Houston 4 San Antonio 2
Roster:

Willie Anderson
Cory Crowder
Terry Cummings
Vinny Del Negro
Howard Eisley
Sean Elliott
Jack Haley
Avery Johnson

Moses Malone
Julius Nwosu
Chuck Person
J. R. Reid
Doc Rivers
David Robinson
Dennis Rodman
Chris Whitney

1995–96
Spurs
Record: 59-23
Head Coach: Bob Hill
League: NBA
Dome: Alamodome
General Manager: Gregg Popovich
Attendance: 811,422
Playoffs: San Antonio 3 Phoenix 1; Utah
        4 San Antonio 2
Roster:

Cory Alexander
Greg Anderson
Vinny Del Negro
Dell Demps
Sean Elliott
Carl Herrera
Avery Johnson
Brad Lohaus

Will Perdue
Chuck Person
J. R. Reid
Doc Rivers
David Robinson
Charles Smith
Monty Williams

1996
Tejanos
Record: 14-14; disbanded while on a road
    trip in Mexico
Head Coach: Joe Cortez
League: Circuito Mexicano de
    Basketball
Gym: Various gymnasiums
Owner: Apuntia
President: Roy Zuniga

1996-97
Spurs
Record: 20-62
Head Coach: Bob Hill out Dec. 10 (3-15),
   Gregg Popovich in Dec. 11 (17-47).
League: NBA
Dome: Alamodome
Chairman: Peter Holt
General Manager: Gregg Popovich
Attendance: 706,641
Roster:

Cory Alexander	Avery Johnson
Greg Anderson	Tim Kempton
Joe Courtney	Vernon Maxwell
Vinny Del Negro	Gaylon Nickerson
Sean Elliott	Will Perdue
Jamie Feick	David Robinson
Devin Gray	Jason Sasser
Darrin Hancock	Charles Smith
Carl Herrera	Dominique Wilkins
Stephen Howard	Monty Williams

1997–98
Spurs
Record: 56-26
Head Coach: Gregg Popovich
League: NBA
Dome: Alamodome
Chairman: Peter Holt
General Manager: Gregg Popovich
Attendance: 783,455
Playoffs: San Antonio 3 Phoenix 1
   Utah 4 San Antonio 1
Roster:

Cory Alexander	Avery Johnson
Willie Burton	Brad Lohaus
Vinny Del Negro	Will Perdue
Tim Duncan	Chuck Person
Sean Elliott	David Robinson
Reggie Geary	Malik Rose
Carl Herrera	Monty Williams
Jaren Jackson	

1998–99
Spurs
NBA champions
Record: 37-13
Head Coach: Gregg Popovich
League: NBA
Dome: Alamodome
Chairman: Peter Holt

General Manager: Gregg Popovich
Attendance: 527,357
Playoffs: San Antonio 3 Minnesota 1
   San Antonio 4 Los Angeles 0
   San Antonio 4 Portland 0
   San Antonio 4 New York 1
Roster:

Antonio Daniels	Steve Kerr
Tim Duncan	Jerome Kersey
Mario Elie	Gerard King
Sean Elliott	Will Perdue
Jaren Jackson	David Robinson
Avery Johnson	Malik Rose
Andrew Gaze	Brandon Williams

1999–2000
Spurs
Record: 53-29
Head Coach: Gregg Popovich
League: NBA
Dome: Alamodome
Chairman: Peter Holt
General Manager: Gregg Popovich
Attendance: 889,444
Playoffs: Phoenix 3 San Antonio 1
Roster:

Chucky Brown	Steve Kerr
Antonio Daniels	Jerome Kersey
Derrick Dial	Terry Porter
Tim Duncan	David Robinson
Mario Elie	Malik Rose
Sean Elliott	Felton Spencer
Jaren Jackson	Samaki Walker
Avery Johnson	

Bombers
Record: 5-13
League: Southwest Basketball League

2000–01
Spurs
Record: 58-24
Head Coach: Gregg Popovich
League: NBA
Dome: Alamodome
Chairman: Peter Holt
General Manager: Gregg Popovich
Attendance: 913,175
Playoffs: San Antonio 3 Minnesota 1
   San Antonio 4 Dallas 1
   Los Angeles 4 San Antonio 0

Roster:

Derek Anderson	Steve Kerr
Antonio Daniels	Ira Newble
Derrick Dial	Terry Porter
Tim Duncan	David Robinson
Sean Elliott	Malik Rose
Danny Ferry	Shawnelle Scott
Jaren Jackson	Samaki Walker
Avery Johnson	

2001
Bombers
**Southwest Basketball League
  Champions**
Record: 13-2
Head Coach: Johnny Moore
League: Southwest Basketball League
Playoffs: San Antonio 2 Austin 1

2001–02
Spurs
Record: 58-24
Head Coach: Gregg Popovich
League: NBA
Dome: Alamodome
Chairman: Peter Holt
General Manager: Gregg Popovich
Attendance: 906,300
Playoffs: San Antonio 3 Seattle 2; Los
  Angeles 4 San Antonio 1
Roster:

Bruce Bowen	Tony Parker
Mark Bryant	Cherokee Parks
Antonio Daniels	Terry Porter
Tim Duncan	David Robinson
Danny Ferry	Malik Rose
Jason Hart	Charles Smith
Stephen Jackson	Steve Smith
Amal McCaskill	

2002-03
Spurs
NBA Champions
Record: 60-22
Head Coach: Gregg Popovich
League: NBA
Arena: SBC Center
Chairman: Peter Holt
GM: R.C. Buford
Attendance: 736,970
Playoffs: San Antonio 4 Phoenix 2; San
  Antonio 4 Los Angeles 2; San
  Antonio 4 Dallas 2; San Antonio 4
  New Jersey 2
Roster:

Mengke Bateer	Stephen Jackson
Bruce Bowen	Steve Kerr
Devin Brown	Tony Parker
Speedy Claxton	David Robinson
Tim Duncan	Malik Rose
Danny Ferry	Steve Smith
Emanuel Ginobili	Kevin Willis

Records, Honors, Exhibition Games

NBA Division Titles
1977-78 Central
1978-79 Central
1980-81 Midwest
1981-82 Midwest
1982-83 Midwest
1989-90 Midwest
1990-91 Midwest
1994-95 Midwest
1995-96 Midwest
1998-99 Midwest
2000-01 Midwest
2001-02 Midwest
2002-03 Midwest

NBA MVP
1994-95 David Robinson
2001-02 Tim Duncan

2002-03 Tim Duncan

NBA Finals MVP
1999 Tim Duncan
2003 Tim Duncan

NBA All-Star Game MVP
1980 George Gervin
2000 Tim Duncan (co-MVP)

NBA Defensive Player of the Year
1985-86 Alvin Robertson
1991-92 David Robinson

NBA All-Defensive First Team
1986-87 Alvin Robertson
1990-91 David Robinson
1991-92 David Robinson

1994-95 David Robinson, Dennis Rodman
1995-96 David Robinson
1998-99 Tim Duncan
1999-00 Tim Duncan
2000-01 Tim Duncan
2001-02 Tim Duncan
2002-03 Tim Duncan

ABA/NBA Rookie of the Year

1973-74 Swen Nater
1989-90 David Robinson
1997-98 Tim Duncan

ABA/NBA All-Rookie First Team Honors

1973-74 Swen Nater
1975-76 Mark Olberding
1987-88 Greg Anderson
1988-89 Willie Anderson
1989-90 David Robinson
1997-98 Tim Duncan
2001-02 Tony Parker

Sporting News Coach of the Year

1980-81 Stan Albeck

NBA Coach of the Year

2002-03 Gregg Popovich

ABA/NBA Executive of the Year

1973-74 Jack Ankerson
1977-78 Angelo Drossos
1989-90 Bob Bass

NBA Most Improved Player

1985-86 Alvin Robertson

IBM Award (previously Schick Award)

1989-90 David Robinson
1990-91 David Robinson
1993-94 David Robinson
1994-95 David Robinson
1995-96 David Robinson
2001-02 Tim Duncan

Seagrams Seven Award

1977-78 George Gervin
1978-79 George Gervin

CBS/Chevrolet MVP

1977-78 George Gervin

All-ABA/NBA First Team Honors

1975-76 James Silas
1977-78 George Gervin
1978-79 George Gervin
1979-80 George Gervin
1980-81 George Gervin
1981-82 George Gervin
1990-91 David Robinson
1991-92 David Robinson
1994-95 David Robinson
1995-96 David Robinson
1997-98 Tim Duncan
1998-99 Tim Duncan
1999-00 Tim Duncan
2000-01 Tim Duncan
2001-02 Tim Duncan
2002-03 Tim Duncan

ABA/NBA League Leaders
Scoring

1977-78 George Gervin 27.2
1978-79 George Gervin 29.6
1979-80 George Gervin 33.1
1981-82 George Gervin 32.3
1993-94 David Robinson 29.8

Rebounds

1974-75 Swen Nater 16.4
1990-91 David Robinson 13.0
1993-94 Dennis Rodman 17.3
1994-95 Dennis Rodman 16.8

Assists

1981-82 Johnny Moore 9.6

Steals

1985-86 Alvin Robertson 3.67
1986-87 Alvin Robertson 3.21

Blocked Shots

1975-76 Billy Paultz 3.05
1980-81 George Johnson 3.39
1981-82 George Johnson 3.12
1991-92 David Robinson 4.49

3-Point Field-Goal Percentage

1982-83 Mike Dunleavy .345
2001-02 Steve Smith .472
2002-03 Bruce Bowen .441

Individual Single Season Records

Points: 2585 George Gervin, 1983-84
Rebounds: 1367 Dennis Rodman, 1993-94
Assists: 816 Johnny Moore, 1984-85

Steals: 301 Alvin Robertson, 1985-86
Blocked Shots: 320 David Robinson, 1990-91
3-PT FG Made: 190 Chuck Person, 1995-96

Individual Single Game Records

Points: 71 David Robinson Apr. 24,1994
Rebounds: 32 Dennis Rodman, Jan. 22, 1994
Assists: 24 John Lucas, Apr. 15,1984
Steals: 11 Larry Kenon, Dec. 26,1976
Blocked Shots: 13 George Johnson, Feb. 24,1981
3-PT FG Made: 9 Chuck Person, Dec. 30,1997

Team Records

Wins: 62, 1994-95
Consecutive Wins: 17, 1995-96
Home Wins: 34, 1980-81 & 1989-90
Road Wins: 29, 1994-95

Spurs Career Leaders

Games

987 David Robinson
899 George Gervin
669 Sean Elliott
644 Avery Johnson
540 James Silas
536 Mark Olberding
519 Johnny Moore
492 Coby Dietrick
488 Mike Mitchell
451 Tim Duncan
451 Willie Anderson
433 Vinny Del Negro
414 Mike Gale
399 Larry Kenon
392 Malik Rose
389 Alvin Robertson
380 Artis Gilmore
378 Billy Paultz
361 Terry Cummings
323 Gene Banks

Points

23,602 George Gervin
20,790 David Robinson
10,324 Tim Duncan
9,799 Mike Mitchell
9,659 Sean Elliott
9,219 James Silas
8,248 Larry Kenon

6,486 Avery Johnson
6,285 Alvin Robertson
6,127 Artis Gilmore

Rebounds

10,497 David Robinson
5,548 Tim Duncan
4,841 George Gervin
4,114 Larry Kenon
3,671 Artis Gilmore
3,203 Billy Paultz
3,004 Mark Olberding
2,941 Sean Elliott
2,683 Mike Mitchell
2,523 Terry Cummings

Assists

4,474 Avery Johnson
3,865 Johnny Moore
2,523 George Gervin
2,441 David Robinson
2,162 James Silas
2,094 Alvin Robertson
1,878 Mike Gale
1,875 Willie Anderson
1,700 Sean Elliott
1,566 Vinny Del Negro

Steals

1,388 David Robinson
1,159 George Gervin
1128 Alvin Robertson
1,017 Johnny Moore
803 Mike Gale
712 Avery Johnson
638 Larry Kenon
568 James Silas
522 Sean Elliott
505 Willie Anderson

Blocked Shots

2,954 David Robinson
1,129 Tim Duncan
938 George Gervin
796 Billy Paultz
700 Artis Gilmore
512 George Johnson
316 Greg Anderson
298 Coby Dietrick
279 Willie Anderson
257 Sean Elliott

3-PT FG Made

563 Sean Elliott

457 Chuck Person
280 Jaren Jackson
250 Dale Ellis
236 Terry Porter
205 Vinny Del Negro
162 Vernon Maxwell
158 Antonio Daniels
157 Bruce Bowen
155 Steve Smith

ABA/NBA All-Star Game
Player Representatives

1974 Rich Jones, Swen Nater.
1975 George Gervin, James Silas, Swen Nater.
1976 George Gervin, James Silas, Larry Kenon, Billy Paultz.
1977 George Gervin
1978 George Gervin, Larry Kenon.
1979 George Gervin, Larry Kenon.
1980 George Gervin
1981 George Gervin
1982 George Gervin
1983 George Gervin, Artis Gilmore.
1984 George Gervin
1985 George Gervin
1986 Artis Gilmore, Alvin Robertson.
1987 Alvin Robertson
1988 Alvin Robertson
1990 David Robinson
1991 David Robinson
1992 David Robinson
1993 David Robinson, Sean Elliott.
1994 David Robinson
1995 David Robinson
1996 David Robinson, Sean Elliott.
1998 Tim Duncan, David Robinson.
2000 Tim Duncan, David Robinson.
2001 Tim Duncan, David Robinson.
2002 Tim Duncan
2003 Tim Duncan

Most Head Coach Wins

Gregg Popovich 339-185 .647
Doug Moe 177-135 .567
Stan Albeck 153-93 .622
Larry Brown 153-131 .537

Bob Bass 144-108 .569
Bob Hill 124-58 .681
John Lucas 94-49 .657
Cotton Fitzsimmons 76-88 .463
Tom Nissalke 62-49 .559
Bob Weiss 59-105 .360

Pre-Spurs Pro Games in San Antonio

1971
Oct. 17 Detroit Pistons 112 Houston Rockets 99

1972
Jan. 26 Chicago Bulls 117 Houston Rockets 108
Feb. 2 Houston Rockets 111 Seattle Supersonics 88
Sep. 26 Houston Rockets 127 Atlanta Hawks 113 (exhibition game)
Oct. 25 Los Angeles Lakers 112 Houston Rockets 107
Nov. 4 Houston Rockets 118 Detroit Pistons 108
Nov. 11 Philadelphia 76ers 114 Houston Rockets 112
Nov. 28 Baltimore Bullets 108 Houston Rockets 90
Nov. 29 Houston Rockets 102 Baltimore Bullets 94
Dec. 20 New York Knicks 124 Houston Rockets 102

1973
Jan. 17 Golden State Warriors 123 Houston Rockets 117
Feb. 4 Houston Rockets 130 Buffalo Braves 118
Feb. 6 Houston Rockets 123 Philadelphia 76ers 117
Feb. 21 Houston Rockets 139 Seattle Supersonics 107
March 7 Cleveland Cavaliers 118 Houston Rockets 100
March 27 Houston Rockets 121 Buffalo Braves 111
March 28 Houston Rockets 138 Buffalo Braves 122

10. Hockey Facts and Figures

Teams

1994–95
Iguanas
Record: 37-22-7
Coach: Bill Goldsworthy out Nov. 12 (3-1-1); Sheldon Gorski, Capt. Dale Henry Nov. 12–Nov. 19 (2-3); John Torchetti in Nov. 20 (32-18-6).
League: Central Hockey League
Arena: Freeman Coliseum
Owner: Horn Chen
General Manager: Jim Goodman
Attendance: 181,879
Playoffs: San Antonio 4 Tulsa 3; Wichita 4 San Antonio 2
Roster:

Ron Aubrey	John Klaers
Mark Bernard	Stu Kulak
John Blessman	Bill Peters
Trevor Buchanan	Ken Plaquin
Malcolm Cameron	Brandy Semchuk
Stephen Corfmat	Brian Shantz
Link Gaetz	Dean Shmyr
Sean Goldsworthy	David Shute
Fred Goltz	Chuck Texeira
Sheldon Gorski	Adam Thompson
Ross Harris	Ken Venis
Dale Henry	Mike Williamson
Paul Jackson	Jeff Winstanley
Scott Kelsey	Mark Yannetti

1995–96
Iguanas
Record: 39-17-8
Coach: John Torchetti
League: Central Hockey League
Arena: Freeman Coliseum
Owner: Horn Chen
General Manager: Dan Heisserer
Attendance: 189,137
Playoffs: San Antonio 4 Memphis 2; Oklahoma City 4 San Antonio 3
Roster:

Chris Albert	Ryan Leschasin
Greg Bailey	Jeff Massey
Jamie Bird	Ryan Pisiak
Matt Bowden	Ken Plaquin
Trevor Buchanan	Darryl Sangster
Gord Christian	Brandy Semchuk
Andrew Gagnon	Brian Shantz
Liam Garvey	David Shute
Tim Green	Jim Sprott
Dale Henry	Rob Weingartner
Mark Hilton	Mike Williams
Paul Jackson	Mark Yannetti
Sebastien LaPlante	Dean Zayonce

1996–97
Iguanas
Record: 26-36-4
Coach: Dale Henry out Jan. 3 (9-24-3), Ric Seiling in Jan. 4 (17-12-1).
League: Central Hockey League
Arena: Freeman Coliseum
Owner: Horn Chen, Ray Miron, Monte Miron
General Manager: Dan Heisserer
Attendance: 96,512
Roster:

Chris Albert	Patrick Larose
Carlos Assayag	Dave Lylyk
Ron Aubrey	Mark Macera
Greg Bailey	Steve Magnusson
Matt Bowden	Don Margettie
Dampy Brar	Jeff Massey
Darcy Cahill	Mike Mychalyshyn
Brent Convery	Jim Peters
Michel Couvrette	Steve Phillips
Don Dwyer	Ryan Pisiak
Brent Fleetwood	Jim Popa
Andrew Gagnon	Steve Pottie
Trent Gleason	Curtis Sayler
Fred Goltz	Brandy Semchuk
Shawn Hall	Jason Smith
Jason Helbing	Jim Sprott
Dale Henry	Kevin St.Pierre
Mike Hiebert	Paul Tompkins
Dean Hulett	Gattis Tseplis

Paul Jackson   Daniel Villeneuve
Travis Kirby   Rob Wilson
Sebastien LaPlante   Mark Yannetti

1996–97
Dragons
Record: 45-30-7
Coach: Jeff Brubaker
League: International Hockey League
Arena: Freeman Coliseum
Owner: Don Levin, Bruce Saurs
President: Jim Goodman
General Manager: Jeff Brubaker
Attendance: 202,171
Playoffs: San Antonio 3 Chicago 1;
   Houston 4 San Antonio 1
Roster:

Len Barrie	Neal Martin
Phil Bergen	Dennis Maxwell
Drake Berehowsky	Justin McHugh
Brent Bilodeau	Jason Miller
Rene Chapdelaine	Brantt Myhres
Mark DeSantis	Darryl Noren
Scott Fraser	Lee Norwood
Brian Glynn	Keith Osborne
David Harlock	Ronalds Ozolinsh
Jon Hillebrandt	Grigori Panteleev
Scott Hollis	Bruce Racine
Ron Hoover	Shawn Reid
Joey Kocur	Todd Reirden
Marc Laforge	Howie Rosenblatt
Brad Layzell	Daniel Shank
Guy Leveque	Brian Shantz
David Littman	Sergei Stas
Lonnie Loach	Brian Sullivan
Dave MacIntyre	Janis Tomans
Darren Maloney	Jean-Guy Trudel
Craig Martin	

1997–98
Dragons
Record: 25-49-8
Coach: Jeff Brubaker
League: International Hockey League
Arena: Freeman Coliseum
Owners: Bruce Saurs, Don Levin
President: Craig Jenkins
General Manager: Jeff Brubaker
Attendance: 150,388
Roster:

Micah Aivazoff	Jason MacIntyre

Dave Archibald	Kurt Mallett
Scott Bailey	Dean Mando
Darren Banks	Craig Martin
Len Barrie	Dennis Maxwell
Luc Beausoleil	Brad Miller
Jason Bonsignore	Grigori Panteleev
Ilya Byakin	Steve Passmore
Rene Chapdelaine	Davis Payne
Dave Chyzowski	Hugo Proulx
Mike Craig	John Purves
Brent Cullaton	Bruce Racine
Kimbi Daniels	Eldon Reddick
Louie DeBrusk	Todd Reirden
Mark DeSantis	Shawn Rivers
Steve Gibson	Andy Roach
Tim Green	Eric Rud
Scott Hollis	Darren Rumble
Ron Hoover	Reggie Savage
Grant Jennings	Daniel Shank
Darin Kimble	Dave Smith
Chris LiPuma	Mike Torchia
Lonnie Loach	Richard Uniacke
Eric Long	Chris Winnes
Dan Lupo	Sergei Zvyagin
Dave MacIntyre	

1998–99
Iguanas
Record: 37-26-7
Coach: Todd Gordon
League: Central Hockey League
Arena: Freeman Coliseum
Owner: Dave Elmore
President: Burl Yarbrough
General Manager: Dave Oldham
Attendance: 127,619
Playoffs: San Antonio 3 Wichita 1;
   Oklahoma City 4 San Antonio 0
Roster:

Johnny Brdarovic	Kevin Lune
Pat Caron	Jason MacIntyre
Levi Clegg	Trevor Matschke
Trevor Converse	Don McGrath
Jason Desjardins	Andy Meth
Philippe DeRouville	Nick Ouimet
Tony Deynzer	Jay Pylypuik
Dave Doucette	Blair Rota
Dave Dow	Warren Sachs
Fred Goltz	Brian Shantz
Roy Gray	Ken Shepard
Scott Green	Paul Taylor

John Hultberg
Paul Jackson
Ricky Jacob
Marc Laforge
Cheyne Lazar
Mike Legg
Mike Loach

Mike Tobin
Rhett Trombley
Gatis Tseplis
Scott Usmail
Steve Wagg
Scott Wray

1999–2000
Iguanas
Record: 33-32-5
Coach: Chris Stewart
League: Central Hockey League
Arena: Freeman Coliseum
Owner: Dave Elmore
General Manager: Dave Oldham
Attendance: 174,201
Roster:

Greg Ambrose
Trevor Anderson
Jeff Boettger
Serge Bourgeois
Johnny Brdarovic
Troy Caley
Craig Coxe
Rhett Dudley
Ryan Edwards
Sam Fields
Martin Fillion
Wade Gibson
Fred Goltz
Scott Green
Ryan Hartung
Ricky Jacob
Garnet Jacobson
Henry Kuster
Marc Laforge
Andrei Lupandin

Dave Lylyk
Tom MacDonald
Jason MacIntyre
Trevor Matschke
Jason Pain
Shawn Penn
Ian Perkins
Denis Pigolitsin
Ryan Pisiak
Michael Pozzo
Tyler Quiring
Blair Rota
Corwin Saurdiff
Brian Shantz
Mitch Shawara
Gatis Tseplis
Scott Usmail
Bob Westerby
Jarret Zukiwsky

2000–01
Iguanas
Record: 42-21-7
Coach: Chris Stewart
League: Central Hockey League
Arena: Freeman Coliseum
Owner: Dave Elmore
General Manager: Rick Carden
Attendance: 154,057
Playoffs: San Antonio 3 Topeka 1;
    Oklahoma City 3 San Antonio 2
Roster:

Aaron Boh

Henry Kuster

Johnny Brdarovic
Paul Buczkowski
Debb Carpenter
Marion Csorich
Darcy Dallas
Jonathan DuBois
Ryan Edwards
Mark Falkowski
Rob Galatiuk
Greg Gatto
Joey Gray
Scott Green
Nathan Grobins
Craig Hayden
Garnet Jacobson

Andrei Lupandin
Michael Marostega
Dale Masson
Marty Melnychuk
Mike Moran
Jeff Parrott
Ian Perkins
Tyler Quiring
Ken Richardson
Nathan Rocheleau
Brian Shantz
Chris Smith
Jeff Trembecky
Derek Watson
Peter Zurba

2001–02
Iguanas
Record: 40-16-8
Coach: Chris Stewart
League: Central Hockey League
Arena: Freeman Coliseum
Owner: Dave Elmore
General Manager: Rick Carden
Attendance: 151,465
Playoffs: Austin 3 San Antonio 1
Roster:

Clay Awe
Brent Belecki
Johnny Brdarovic
Matt Carmichael
Mark DeSantis
Jonathan Dubois
Ryan Edwards
Rob Galatiuk
Greg Gatto
Pat Glenday
Joey Gray

Scott Green
Russell Hogue
Matt Van Horlick
Marek Jass
Henry Kuster
Jim Lawrence
Blair Manning
Jeff Parrott
Scott Reid
Ken Richardson
Darby Walker

2002–03
Rampage
Record: 36-29-11-4
Coach: John Torchetti out Mar. 6 (30-23-
    10-2), Scott Allen in Mar. 7 (6-6-1-2)
League: American Hockey League
Arena: SBC Center
Chairman: Peter Holt
General Manager: John Torchetti
Attendance: 201,490
Playoffs: Norfolk 3 San Antonio 0
Roster:

Eric Beaudoin

Sean O'Connor

Mathieu Biron
Jim Campbell
Pierre Dagenais
Paul Elliott
Wade Flaherty
Sean Gagnon
Tyrone Garner
David Gove
Mike Green
Ryan Jardine

Josh Olson
Serge Payer
Michel Periard
Andy Reierson
Byron Ritchie
Jamie Rivers
Kyle Rossiter
Vladimir Sapozhnikov
Eric Schneider
Denis Shvidki

Scott Kelman
Juraj Kolnik
Lukas Krajicek
Simon Lajeunesse
Andy Lundbohm
Chris Mason
Stephane Matteau
Branislav Mezei
David Morisset
Filip Novak

Matt Smith
Joey Tetarenko
Rocky Thompson
Jeff Toms
Pascal Trepanier
Igor Ulanov
Mike Van Ryn
Mike Vellinga
Brendan Walsh

Records, Honors, Exhibition Games

Individual Records–Players

Games: 292 Brian Shantz
Goals: 186 Paul Jackson
Assists: 329 Brian Shantz
Points: 489 Brian Shantz

Individual Records–Goaltending

Wins: 42 Mike Williams
Shutouts: 6 Bruce Racine

Player Representatives, All-Star Game

1998-99 Johnny Brdarovic, Dave
  Doucette, Paul Jackson, Brian Shantz.
1999-2000 Brian Shantz
2000-01 Paul Buczkowski, Scott Green.
2001-02 Jonathan DuBois, Mark
  DeSantis, Blair Manning.
2002-03 Filip Novak

Single-Season Individual Records

Goals: 56 Johnny Brdarovic, 1998-99
  Iguanas
Assists: 85 Brian Shantz, 1995-96
  Iguanas
Points: 139 Brian Shantz, 1995-96
  Iguanas
Goaltending Wins: 27 Mike Williams,
  1995-96 Iguanas
Goals Against Average: 2.03 Matt
  Carmichael, 2001-02 Iguanas

Shutouts: 6 Bruce Racine, 1996-97 Dragons

MVP Award

1994-95 Paul Jackson
1995-96 Brian Shantz

Rookie of the Year

1998-99 Johnny Brdarovic

All-Rookie Team

2002-03 Filip Novak

Coach of the Year

1994-95 John Torchetti

Most Head Coach Wins

Chris Stewart 115-69-20
John Torchetti 101-58-16-10
Jeff Brubaker 70-79-15
Todd Gordon 37-26-7
Ric Seiling 17-12-1

Exhibition Games

1994
Sep. 27 Dallas Stars 3 Los Angeles
  Kings 2
2003
Sep. 27 San Antonio 2 Florida Panthers 1

Training Camp

2003 Florida Panthers

11. Boxing Facts and Figures

Fights in San Antonio

1896
Jim Corbett and Bob Fitzsimmons train in San Antonio

1920
Mar. 11 Otto "Young" Wallace Bob Waugh W 10
Nov. 23 Jack Britton Bud Logan W 10
Dec. 28 Young Fitzsimmons Jack Dillon W 12

1921
Nov. 5 Young Dempsey Kid Pancho NC 10
Dec. 1 Johnny "Young" Rosner Kid Pancho NC 10

1922
Jan. 1 Johnny "Young" Rosner Kid Pancho NC 10
Feb. 14 Kid Pancho Bobby Hughes W 10
May 22 Johnny McCoy Kid Pancho W 10
Jun. 5 Johnny McCoy Tim O'Dowd D 12
Oct. 3 Johnny McCoy Dale Hill W 12
Oct. 16 Johnny McCoy Tim O'Dowd W 12
Nov. 2 Johnny McCoy Frankie Mason NC 9
Dec. 27 Sam Langford Son Goodrich KO 5

1923
Feb. 20 Johnny McCoy Babe Asher W 10
Mar. 6 Johnny McCoy Eddie Connors W 10
Aug. 21 Kid Pancho Gene LaRue TKO 3
Sep. 4 Gene LaRue Kid Pancho NC 4
Sep. 17 Kid Pancho Gene LaRue KO 3

Nov. 26 Johnny McCoy Jackie Feldman W 12
Dec. 21 Son Goodrich Sam Langford W 10

1924
Jan. 31 Tiger Flowers Son Goodrich W 12
Feb. 26 Newsboy Brown Kid Pancho W 12
Mar. 4 Kid Pancho Newsboy Brown D 12
Mar. 25 Billy McCann Tommy White NC 12

Apr. 15 Pascal Colletti Kid Pancho KO 4
Jun. 3 Kid Pancho Jackie Doyle KO 6

1926
Nov. 12 Kid Pancho Billy Tingle KO 3

1927
Jan. 4 Kid Pancho Kid Suarez KO 3
Apr. 13 Kid Lencho Jimmy McDermott D 10
Jun. 14 Harold Smith Kid Lencho NC 10; David Velasco Mickey Young W 10
Jun. 28 Brooks Hooper Battling Shaw W 4
Jul. 12 Kid Pancho Johnny McCoy D 10
Battling Shaw Terry Young W 4
Jul. 28 Battling Shaw Young Pancho KO 2
Aug. 2 Johnny McCoy Kid Pancho W 10
Aug. 19 Johnny McCoy Marcial Zavala W 10
Aug. 30 Battling Shaw Kid George W 6
Sep. 28 Battling Shaw Kid George W 6
Oct. 1 Battling Shaw Terry Young KO 5
Oct. 9 Sergeant Sammy Baker Pete Aug. TKO 6
Oct. 11 Kid Laredo Alberto Arizmendi D 10
Dick Wymore Don Coll KO 3
Oct. 18 Carlos Garcia Dick Wymore TKO 9
Nov. 10 Battling Shaw Kid George W 6
Dec. 10 Battling Shaw Kid Torreno W 6
Dec. 12 Battling Shaw Kid Torreno KO 4
Dec. 20 Carlos Garcia Willie Pedraza W 10
Bobby Brown Jimmy Hernandez KO 2

1928
Jan. 1 Alberto Arizmendi Caveman Ferrici W 10
Jan. 10 Battling Shaw Newsboy Reyes W 6
Feb. 1 Battling Shaw Terry Young KO 2
Feb. 7 Johnny Hughes Kid Fernandez W 10
Feb. 10 Battling Shaw Newsboy Reyes W 6
Feb. 28 Battling Shaw George Marcus KO 3
Mar. 6 Alberto Arizmendi Battling Herrera KO 5; Mike Vasquez Chico Cisneros D 10
Mar. 10 Battling Shaw Joe Montoya W 6
Mar. 28 Alberto Arizmendi Newsboy

Reyes W 6
Apr. 1 Battling Shaw Joe Montoya KO 4
Apr. 4 Battling Shaw Joe Montoya KO 2
Apr. 10 Kid Adams Alberto Arizmendi D 6
May 10 Battling Shaw Kid Monterrey W 6
May 22 Alberto Arizmendi Kid Adams W 8
Jun. 10 Battling Shaw Juan Hernandez W 6
Jul. 1 Battling Shaw Kid Malabonos KO 5
Jul. 2 Alberto Arizmendi Kid Adams W 8
Jul. 9 Alberto Arizmendi Al Bosque W 4
Jul. 24 Bobby Fernandez Honeyboy
  Snipes W 10
Jul. 26 Chico Cisneros Jimmy Watts D 10
Aug. 1 Battling Shaw Mickey Cromwell KO 6
Aug. 27 Kid Adams Billy Kane W 4
Sep. 4 Martin Burke Jack League NC 10
Sep. 13 Kid Cober Battling Shaw KO 6
Oct. 9 Sergeant Sammy Baker Pete Aug.
  KO 6; Jimmy McDermott Kid Pancho
Nov. 10 Battling Shaw Pablo Alejandro W 6
Dec. 10 Battling Shaw Sailor Barrera W 10
Dec. 12 Battling Shaw Kid Macey W 10

1929
Jan. 10 Battling Shaw Kid Pancho W 10
Jan. 15 Kid Pancho Battling Shaw D 10
Feb. 1 Battling Shaw Kid Pancho KO 9
Feb. 10 Battling Shaw Kid Pancho W 10
Feb. 12 Battling Shaw Mickey Cromwell KO 7
  Paul Wangley Carlos Garcia KO 3
Mar. 5 Carlos Garcia Paul Wangley W 10
Mar. 15 Del Wildcat Monte Batlling Shaw
  D 10
Mar. 23 Brooks Harper Battling Shaw D 10

1932
Dec. 29 Primo Carnera Jack League W 6

1933
Mar. 20 Tommy Monroe Joe White KO 2;
  Kid Williams Mike Martinez W 6;
  Robert Gomez Kid Bruno W 6; Henry
  Moreno Kid Carmona W 6
Aug. 2 Chuck Burns Champ Clark KO 8
Aug. 31 Texas legalizes boxing.
Sep. 19 Maxie Chuck Burns W 10
Dec. 6 Willard Brown Midget Mexico W 10

1934
Jan. 3 Midget Mexico Roy Calamira W 10
Jan. 9 Cecilio Lozada Midget Mexico TKO 5

Jan. 16 Midget Mexico Roy Calamira W 10
Jan. 23 Cecilio Lozada Midget Mexico W 10
Feb. 20 Wild Bill McDowell Red Hughes W 6
Mar. 6 Wild Bill McDowell Red Hughes KO 3
Mar. 13 Wild Bill McDowell Al Leuschner KO 3
Mar. 20 Bobby Batllia Wild Bill McDowell W 8
Mar. 26 Midget Mexico Eddie Anderson W
  10; Wild Bill McDowell Johnny Paige TKO 1
Apr. 2 Tracy Cox Cecilio Lozada KO1
Apr. 3 Wild Bill McDowell Joe Murray KO 1
Apr. 6 Midget Mexico Frankie Graham W 10
Apr. 9 Tracy Cox Jack Gagnon KO1
Apr. 10 Wild Bill McDowell Dell Hawkins W 8
Apr. 16 Tracy Cox Manuel Zermanio KO1
Apr. 17 Wild Bill McDowell Jack Kay W 8
Apr. 30 Wild Bill McDowell Young Sena W 6
May 7 Cecilio Lozada Wild Bill McDowell
  W 10
Jun. 19 Tracy Cox Joe Ruiz KO 5
Sep. 4 Midget Mexico Paul Gritta W 10;
  Augie Arellano Wild Bill McDowell KO 4
Sep. 11 Pelon Lopez Midget Mexico D 10
Oct. 16 Midget Mexico Ray "Kid" Kiser W 10
Oct. 23 Midget Mexico Spud kelly KO 3
Nov. 1 Midget Mexico Pelon Lopez W 10

1935
Jan. 17 Midget Mexico Tony O'Dell W 10
Jan. 29 Tracy Cox Midget Mexico W 10
Feb. 5 Wild Bill McDowell Elias Alvarez W 6
Feb. 14 Wild Bill McDowell Young Senna W 6
Feb. 15 Tracy Cox Midget Mexico TKO 10
Feb. 19 Wild Bill McDowell Tony Eqarias W 6
Feb. 26 Wild Bill McDowell Francis
  Cunningham W 6
Mar. 12 Wild Bill McDowell Joe White W 6
Apr. 9 Midget Mexico Wild Bill McDowell W 10
Apr. 16 Midget Mexico Louis Beard DQ 9
May 21 Midget Mexico Lou Jallos W 10;
  Wild Bill McDowell Tommy Collins W 6
Jun. 18 Midget Mexico Louis Beard KO 3
Jun. 20 Ralph Sikes Wild Bill McDowell W 10
Jun. 26 Baby Manuel Kid Laredo KO 4
Jul. 2 Baby Manuel Jackie Griffin KO 9
Jul. 10 Kid Barrilito Baby Manuel D 10

1936
Jun. 24 Max Baer Wilson Dunn KO 3
Jul. 16 Tracy Cox K. O. Castillo KO6
Dec. 14 Wiilard Brown Midget Mexico D
  10; Kid Azteca Tracy Cox W 10

1938
Nov. 28 Kid Azteca Billy Deeg W 10
Dec. 16 Kid Azteca Kenny Lasalle W 10
Dec. 23 Pedro Ortega Lew Jenkins W 8

1939
Jan. 20 Kid Azteca Eddie McGeever W 10
Feb. 3 Kid Azteca Eddie McGeever KO 8
May 15 Juan Zurita Jimmy "Kid" Hatcher W 10, wins Mexico's featherweight title
Jun. 19 Lew Jenkins Jorge Morelia W 10; Gabriel Rocha Wild Bill McDowell W 10

1940
Dec. 13 Kid Azteca Bobby Pacho D 10; Juan Zurita Nick Peters W 10

1941
Apr. 8 Juan Zurita Lloyd Pine W 10

1943
Feb. 15 Amado Rodriguez Midget Mexico D 10

1944
Sep. 12 Fritzie Zivic Felix Oreles KO 2
Oct. 17 Juan Zurita Aldo Spoldi KO 4
Dec. 12 Fritzie Zivic Kid Azteca W 10
1945
Jan. 23 Juan Zurita Paul Altman KO 5
Apr. 3 Fritzie Zivic Manuel Villa KO 8
May 7 Fritzie Zivic Kid Azteca W 10
Proctor Heinhold Jose Mendoza W 8
May 22 Proctor Heinhold Chu Chu Llanes W 10
Jun. 12 Fritzie Zivic Baby Zavala KO 4
Jun. 13 Fritzie Zivic James Hall Exh 3
Aug. 14 Tony Elizondo Ben Johnson W 6
Aug. 28 Tony Elizondo Billy Deerling KO 3
Sep. 11 Tony Elizondo Johnny Riley KO 3
Sep. 24 Tony Mar Maurice LaChance KO 3
Tony Elizondo Steve Latz KO 1
Nov. 6 Tony Elizondo Paul Altman KO 1
Nov. 20 Manuel Ortiz Proctor Heinhold W 10

1946
Feb. 5 Tony Elizondo Artie Dorrell W 10
Mar. 19 Julio Rodriguez Jimmy Curl KO 3
Mar. 26 Tony Elizondo Fritzie Zivic W 10
Mar. 27 Arturo Godoy Johnny Denson KO 5

Apr. 2 Enrique Bolanos Georgie Hansford KO 2
Apr. 4 Bobby Dykes Jose Macias W 6
Apr. 30 Tony Elizondo Danny Rosati DQ 4
Pelon Garcia Jimmy Curl W 6
May 5 Fernando Sosa Bobby Dykes W 6
Jun. 4 Tony Elizondo Paul Altman W 10
Jun. 6 Bobby Dykes Joe Perales W 6
Aug. 27 Tony Elizondo Jimmy Curl W 10
Sep. 17 Bobby Dykes Jesus Rodriguez W 4
Sep. 24 Bobby Dykes Juan Zapata KO 3
Oct. 29 Bobby Dykes Joe Maccas W 4
Nov. 12 Tony Elizondo Bobby Britton W 10

1947
Jan. 7 Jimmy Curl Baby Yucatan KO 4
Mar. 11 Bobby Dykes Antonio Aznar KO 6; Jimmy Curl Amado Rodriguez KO 6
Apr. 1 Vincente Villavicencio Tony Elizondo KO 2
Jun. 17 Bobby Dykes Fred Gonzalez KO 2; Jimmy Curl Vincente Villavicencio KO 7
Jul. 1 Bobby Dykes Gillermo Pardo KO 3
Sep. 1 Bobby Dykes Manuel Girces W 6
Sep. 9 Joe Scott John C Curtis D 4
Oct. 7 Jackie Blair Jesus Rodriguez W 6
Oct. 21 Enrique Bolanos Tony Rios KO 5
Nov. 4 Jackie Blair Johnny Villanueva W 6
Nov. 25 Bobby Dykes Chango Patino KO 4
Jimmy Curl Bob Castro W 10
Dec. 2 Jackie Blair Reynaldo Ramon W 6

1948
Jan. 6 Jose Cardenas Jackie Blair D 6
May 6 Choforo Martinez Bobby Dykes D 10
Jun. 22 Jimmy Curl Ernie Rios KO 7
Jul. 27 Jackie Blair Alvaro Estrada W 8
Aug. 17 Jimmy Curl Babe Zavala KO 1
Sep. 14 Charley Salas Bert Linam W 10
Oct. 26 Joe Brown Frank Cockrell KO 5

1949
Mar. 16 Bobby Dykes Charley Salas W 10
Aug. 2 Jimmy Curl Tommy Ramirez W 10
Aug. 29 Jimmy Curl Tony Johnson W 10

1950
Oct. 30 Jackie Blair Valentine Luna W 10
Nov. 8 Sugar Ray Robinson Bobby Dykes W 10 in Chicago
Nov. 27 Bobby Dykes Jose Rocha KO 3

1951

Jan. 8 Jackie Blair Jesus Alonzo KO 6
Apr. 10 Bobby Dykes Nick Moran W 10;
  Jackie Blair Rudy DeHoyos W 8
May 22 Jackie Blair Lauro Salas W
  10,Texas lightweight title
Aug. 7 IH Sporty Harvey Doug Watters KO 4

1952

Feb. 4 Kid Gavilan Bobby Dykes W 15 in
  Miami,FL; Galivan retains World
  Welterweight title
Feb. 19 IH Sport Harvey John Victor
  Penn W 8
Jun. 17 Bobby Dykes Pete Gil KO 6
Sep. 23 Bobby Dykes Cisco Saenz KO 8
Sep. 28 Jackie Blair Babe Barrada KO 3
Oct. 7 IH Sporty Harvey Archie Collins KO 3
Oct. 20 IH Sporty Harvey Bob Dixon W 4
Nov. 11 IH Sporty Harvey Bob Dixon KO 4
Nov. 25 George Bebelle IH Sporty
  Harvey W 6
Dec. 30 IH Sporty Harvey Stan Jones W 4

1953

Feb. 10 Willie Pep Jose Alvarez W 10
Mar. 2 Bobby Dykes Joe Arthur W 10
  Eddie Brant Al Juergens W 10
Mar. 10 Del Flanagan Chato Hernandez W 10
Mar. 12 Jimmy Martinez Jesse Fuentes W 10
Mar. 23 Al Juergens Eddie Brant TKO 8
Apr. 2 Bobby Dykes Jimmy Martinez W 10
Apr. 28 Jimmy Martinez Del Flanagan W 10
  Jimmy Curl Eloy Vann KO 1
Jul. 21 Pappy Gault Alex Santoy W 10
Sep. 14 Stan Jones IH Sporty Harvey W 6
Nov. 24 Alvin Williams Joe Moran W 12

1954

Mar. 30 Tom Busby Dick Cole KO 2
Apr. 6 IH Sporty Harvey Jimmy Bryant KO 3
Sep. 28 Celso Hidalgo Henry Miramontes
  W 6; Harold Jones El Conscripto KO 2
Nov. 9 Cesar Saavedra Babe Mathias W 10
  Henry Miramontes Celso Hidalgo W 6
Nov. 23 Willie Pastrano Bobby Dykes W
  10 in Miami,FL
Nov. 30 Pirrin Vega Harold Jones D 10

1955

Feb. 24 Buddy Turman IH Harvey W 10

in Dallas; San Antonio native Harvey
first black boxer to face a white boxer in
Texas
Mar. 8 Manuel Armenteros Joe Boland W 10
Mar. 16 Bobby Dykes Kid Gavilan W 10
  in Miami
Mar. 28 Manuel Armenteros Teddy
  Roberts W 10
Apr. 12 Manuel Armenteros Otilio Galvan W 10
Apr. 26 IH Sporty Harvey Jesus Alonzo W 6
May 12 Raul "Raton" Macias Baby Moe
  Morio TKO 5
Jun. 7 Chebo Hernandez Norris Burse W 10
Jul. 7 Bobby Dykes Moses Ward W 10
Jul. 12 Baby Vasquez Georgie Collins W 10
Jul. 21 Billy Peacock Oscar Torres W 10
Aug. 9 Ramon Fuentes Al Juergens W 10
Aug. 16 Bobby Dykes Chebo Hernandez
  KO 4

1956

Jan. 10 Ernie Ramos Curt Woolwine W 6
May 22 Willie Pep Manuel Armenteros
  TKO 7; Danny Cardenas Maxie Trero W 8
Sep. 22 Jesse Rodriguez Jose Gonzalez
  W 10; Rocky Marciano was referee;
  Ray Riojas Henry Johnson KO 3
Nov. 1 Kid Anahuac Carmen Iacobucci KO 3
Nov. 13 Ray Riojas Jackie Blair W 12
Nov. 21 Raul "Raton" Macias Gaetano
  Annaloro W 10

1957

Feb. 12 Jimmy McCoy Gil Tapia W 6;
  Santiago Gutierrez Phil McCoy W 6
Mar. 19 Eloy Vann Alvin Williams KO 5;
  Frank Valdez Gino Tovar W 4
May 14 Jesse Gutierrez Ray Gonzales D 6
Jul. 30 Joe Brown Gilberto Holguin W
  10; Frank Valdez JD Laird KO 4
  Norris Burse Matt Jackson D 6;
  George Peyton Eloy Vann KO 7
Aug. 27 Matt Jackson George Peyton W
  8; Rocky Morales Calvin Carney KO 2
Oct. 8 Barbara Buttrick Phyllis Kugler UD 6

1958

Sep. 16 Larry Baker David Cervantes W 10

1959

Jan. 9 Gene Fullmer Milo Savage W 10;

Alfredo Zuany Leo Parks KO 2
Jan. 12 Tony Montano Mickey Brown W 10
Apr. 14 Alfredo Zuany Matt Jackson W 10
May 19 Battling Torres Russ Tague KO 3
Sep. 8 Lauro Salas Frank Valdez D 10
Sep. 22 Tod Herring Charlie Roberts W 4; Mel Barker Joe Miceli TD 2
Sep. 23 Alejandro Lavorante Dean C Bogany KO 3
Oct. 20 Alejandro Lavorante Sherman Goodman KO 2
Nov. 24 Joey Archer Aman Peck W 10; Tod Herring Abe Lewis KO 2; Roy Harris Alejandro Lavorante W 10
Dec. 1 Manuel Gonzalez Rogelio Sandoval KO 3

1960
Jan. 26 Eloy Vann Benny Davison W 8
Feb. 16 Manuel Gonzalez Joe Louis Hargrove KO 7
Mar. 15 Jose Becerra Ward Yee W 10
Mar. 21 Ray Portilla Joe Brown TKO 7; Alejandro Lavorante Garvin Sawyer KO 2; Roy Harris Henry Hall W 7
Apr. 5 Manuel Gonzalez Garland "Rip" Randall W 10
May 16 Frank Valdez Gallito Reyes KO 8
Aug. 22 S Gutierrez Karl Heinz Guder W 10
Aug. 23 Alonso Witherspoon Willis Earls D 4

1961
Jan. 31 Jesse Leija Bobby Bell KO 1
Feb. 14 Torito Mota Luis Leija W 10
Mar. 7 Alonso Witherspoon Leonard Mitchell TKO 4
Mar. 21 Alejandro Lavorante Tunney Hunsaker KO 5; Jose Medel Herman Marques W 12; Luis Leija Torito Mota W 10
Apr. 11 Willie Ramos Jose Luiz Amador D 4
May 16 Jose Soto Benjamin Armstrong TKO 3
Jun. 16 Kenny Lane Ray Portilla KO 6
Jul. 14 Sixto San Miguel Rocky Randell W 10
Aug. 18 Manuel Gonzalez Henry Watson W 10; Al Gonzalez Leo Bennett KO 1
Aug. 25 Herman Duncan Juan Ramirez W 10
Sep. 14 Luis Leija Jorge "Baby" Salazar D 10
Sep. 29 Humberto Barrera Jesus Alaniz

KO 4; Gaspar Ortega Kid Rayo W 10
Oct. 17 Humberto Barrera Mague Jasso KO 2
Nov. 14 Humberto Barrera Artie Clark KO 8
Nov. 28 Frankie Ramirez Gaspar Ortega W 10
Dec. 4 Luis Leija Chamaco Perez W 10 Humberto Barrera Chamaco Martinez W 8
Dec. 11 Humberto Barrera Alberto Cortez W 8

1962
Jan. 16 Javier Ovalle Sylvan Carlin KO 6; Humberto Barrera Nacho Escalante W 10
Feb. 13 Curtis Cokes Kid Rayo W 10
Feb. 21 Porfirio Zamora Lalo Hernandez W 4; Humberto Barrera Luis Leija W 10
Mar. 28 Porfirio Zamora Daniel Lopez KO 3
Apr. 10 Chato Herrera Porfirio Zamora D 6
Jul. 24 Charlie Roberts Jose Soto KO 5; Jose "Toluco II" Lopez Miguel Hernandez KO 3
Aug. 21 Battling Torres Art Hayward KO 9
Sep. 14 Porfirio Zamora Manuel Ochoa KO 3; Humberto Barrera Chamaco Perez W 10
Oct. 30 Battling Torres Joey Parks KO 3
Nov. 6 Luis Rodriguez Santiago Gutierrez KO 3
Nov. 13 Johnny Brooks Rogelio Reyes W 4; Cuervo Salinas Humerto Barrera W 10
Dec. 4 Miguel Hernandez Porfirio Zamora D 8
Dec. 11 Davey Moore Fili Nava W 10

1963
Jan. 15 Porfirio Zamora Miguel Hernandez KO 3; Humberto Barrera Jose Cejudo W 10
Jan. 29 Porfirio Zamora Alfred Franklin W 8; Humberto Barrera Cuervo Salazar W 10
Feb. 5 Sonny Moore Al Gonzalez KO 3
Mar. 13 Porfirio Zamora Jessie Alaniz KO 5
Apr. 1 Porfirio Zamora Antonio Martinez W 8; Humberto Barrera Jorge Salazar W 10
Apr. 16 Santiago Gutierrez Del Flanagan KO 7; Porfirio Zamora Ruben Herrera KO 5
May 14 Manny Elias Humberto Barrera TKO 9
Aug. 16 Porfirio Zamora Alfredo Puente KO 1
Oct. 1 Jose Moreno Porfirio Zamora W 10
Oct. 21 Porfirio Zamora Freddie Burris KO 3

Dec. 1 Chucho Garcia Azbache Aguilar KO 3
Dec. 17 Porfirio Zamora Beldon Paton W 10

1964

Aug. 21 Billy Marsh Javier Villanueva KO 4 Humberto Barrera Florencio Solente TKO 10
Dec. 16 Porfirio Zamora Henry Dominguez KO 8

1965

May 1 Chucho Garcia Floyd Molina KO 4
Nov. 2 Jerry Quarry Roy Crear KO 3 Benito Juarez Frank Taylor KO 1
Dec. 7 Jose "Pollo" Gabino Porfirio Zamora W 10

1966

Apr. 1 Karl Zurheide Tommy Simms KO 7; Mark Tessman James Smith KO 3; Dave Zyglewicz Max Martinez KO 6
Apr. 12 Oscar Albarado Gennaro Morones KO 4; Ramedez Marquez Cesar Navarez KO 6
Jul. 26 Jesus Pimentel Billy Smith KO 5; Doug Agin Miguel Hernandez KO 8
Oct. 26 Jesus Pimentel Katsuo Saito KO 8

1967

Jun. 11 Yoshio Nakane Jesus Pimentel W 10
Jul. 26 Jesus Pimentel Mimun Ben-Ali TKO 9; Archie Moore was referee; Jose Bisbal Jose Luis Pimentel D 10
Nov. 14 Oscar Albarado Bily Strother W 6; Cowboy Roy Rogers Tony "Kid" Longoria NC 8
Dec. 12 Oscar Albarado Hector Ramirez KO 2; Jesus Pimentel Mike Langlois KO 6; Jose Luis Pimentel Ramon Reyes KO 4

1968

Mar. 19 Oscar Albarado Gilbert Gutierrez W 8; Jesus Pimentel Ray Jutras KO 4
Apr. 2 Oscar Albarado Gilbert Gutierrez KO 1
May 3 Oscar Albarado Gilbert De Los Santos KO 6; Jesus Pimentel Rollie Penaroya TKO 5
Jul. 30 Jose Luis Pimentel Hip-Sang Lee KO 4
Aug. 27 Terry Krueger Sherman Goodwin KO 4; Willis Earls Ed Land KO 5;

Manuel Ramos Marty Franklin KO 4
Sep. 10 Oscar Albarado Cassius Greene KO 1; Terry Krueger John R Jones KO 3
Sep. 30 Oscar Albarado Lonnie Harris KO 1; Willie Warren Rocky Martin KO 8; Terry Krueger Ernest Montez KO 1
Oct. 29 Oscar Albarado Jerry Graci KO 9; Jesus Pimentel Johnny Readone KO 2; Mando Ramos Billy Coleman KO 3
Nov. 13 Chango Carmona Percy Hayles TKO 4
Nov. 19 Efren Torres Jose Salinas KO 1; Jorge Rosales Willie Warren D 10 ; Jerry Quarry Willis Earls W 10; Terry Krueger Andrew Stewart KO 1

1969

Mar. 21 Terry Krueger Lee Powell KO 1
Jun. 3 Oscar Albarado Johnny Brooks KO 7; Terry Krueger Joe Sharlow KO 2; Cesar Deciga Bennie McCall W 10
Jun. 20 Terry Krueger Tony Anchondo KO 1; Art Hernandez Chuck Spencer KO 4; Genaro Soto Chango Carmona D 10
Jul. 15 Manuel Avitia Johnny Brooks W 10
Jul. 29 Jesus Pimentel Rafael Herrera W 10; Terry Krueger Cliff Williams KO 2; Jose Luis Pimentel Gene Young W 10
Sep. 9 Terry Krueger Charlie Roberts KO 1; Chango Carmona Doug Agin KO 2; Arturo Leon Hernandez Carlos Zayas KO 4
Oct. 7 Oscar Albarado L.C. Morgan DQ 5; Terry Krueger Robert Bonner KO 1
Oct. 28 Oscar Albarado L.C. Morgan KO 5; Terry Krueger Sam Harris KO 1
Nov. 11 Raul Rojas Rogelio Tulunghari KO 7; Rodolfo Gonzalez Javier Jimenez KO 6
Nov. 26 John McCluskey Arturo Leon TKO 1
Dec. 2 Terry Krueger Henry Hall KO 6 Max Martinez Arthur Wright W 6
Dec. 9 Oscar Albarado Robert Williams KO 7
Dec. 17 Jesus Pimentel Billy McGrandle KO 7
Dec. 30 Jesus Pimentel Benito Montes KO 2

1970

Jan. 13 Mando Ramos Leonardo Aquero W 10
Feb. 24 Terry Krueger Johnny Jackson KO 1
Mar. 18 Ruben Olivares Romy Guelas TKO 6
Apr. 7 Jose "King" Roman Tommy Grant KO 1
May 7 Terry Krueger Bobby Rascon KO 3

Jun. 16 Jesus Pimentel Kazuyoshi Kanazawa KO 3
Jun. 30 Terry Krueger Max Martinez KO 4; Tony Moreno Roy Mendez W 6
Jul. 17 Raul Montoya Shinichi Kakizawa W 10; Tony Moreno Roger Lopez KO 1
Jul. 28 Tony Moreno Manuel Jimenez KO 1
Aug. 10 Terry Krueger Jose Palookajita KO 1
Aug. 25 Terry Krueger Kame De Kabbajar KO 1
Sep. 11 Tony Moreno Frankie Granados KO 9
Sep. 14 Jesus Pimentel Ushiwakamaru Harada KO 5
Oct. 6 Ray Boyd Gilbert Gutierrez KO 3
Oct. 7 Oscar Albarado Larry Brazier KO 3
Nov. 10 Tony Moreno Raul Noria W 10
Nov. 24 Oscar Albarado Raul Soriano W 10
Dec. 18 Tony Moreno John McCluskey W 10

1971
Jan. 22 Ray Boyd Art Rivera KO 1
Jan. 29 Kenny Weldon Ronnie Bourque KO 1
Feb. 9 Mongol Ortiz Terry Krueger KO 8
Feb. 24 Mongol Ortiz Jimmy Boyde W 10
Mar. 16 Roy Barrientos Modesto Salinas KO 3; Tony Moreno Jose Orantes W 10
Apr. 17 Oscar Albarado Frankie Lewis W 10; Jesus Pimentel Mamoru Minami KO 4; Roy Barrientos Jesse Lara KO 6; Ricardo Garcia Jimmy Trosclair W 10
May 11 Angel Macias Marion Thomas KO 3
Jun. 11 Roy Barrientos Johnny Gonzalez KO 5; Johnny Moreno Mario Perez KO 4
Jun. 18 Masao Ohba Rocky Garcia KO 9
Jun. 22 Jesus Pimentel Modesto Cabrers KO 2
Jun. 29 Mongol Ortiz Terry Krueger W 10
Jul. 2 Roy Barrientos Percy Pugh W 10; Johnny Moreno Jose Reyna KO 1
Jul. 20 Johnny Moreno Ramiro Lopez KO 2
Aug. 27 Gilbert Mares Ray Boyd W 10
Sep. 1 Johnny Moreno Victor Rocha KO 2
Sep. 22 Clyde Brown Jimmy Cross KO 3; Johnny Moreno Jose Orantes KO 8
Oct. 5 Jorge Rosales Willie Warren W 10
Oct. 7 George Foreman Ollie Wilson KO 2; Tony Moreno Roberto Alvarez W 10
Oct. 9 Terry Krueger Clyde Brown KO 1
Nov. 2 Johnny Moreno Chamaco Cuenca W 10

1972
Jan. 14 Tony Moreno Arturo Vazquez KO 2; Johnny Moreno Juan Cantu W 10
Feb. 8 Terry Krueger Clarence Boone KO 2
Mar. 14 Sam Torres Ray Boyd KO 3 Tony Rocha Cisco Reyes W 4
Mar. 21 Sonny Moore Terry Krueger TKO 3
May 1 Ronnie Wright Elgie Walters W 10
May 16 Leoperdo Aguero Johnny Copeland KO 4; Tony Moreno Ricardo Delgado D 10
Jun. 6 Oscar Albarado James Shelton KO 3
Jun. 20 Johnny Moreno Apolino Salinas KO 1
Jul. 11 Oscar Albarado Demetrio Salazar KO 4
Oct. 3 Manuel Elizondo Sam Torres KO 7
Oct. 24 Angel Espada Alfonso Aguirre KO 3; Manuel Elizondo Ernie Burns KO 10
Nov. 14 Cesar Deciga Estanislado Cuenca KO 3; Manuel Elizondo Roy McMillan KO 4

1973
Mar. 16 Terry Krueger Terry Sorrel KO 10
May 15 Tony Moreno Tony Padrone KO 2; Johnny Moreno Rocky Garcia KO 8
May 17 Friolan Martinez Baby Corona KO 3
Jul. 3 Johnny Moreno Tarcisio Gomez W 10
Aug. 28 Tony Rocha Pero Gonzales W 10; Tony Padrone Tony Moreno W 10
Oct. 2 Cesar Deciga Johnny Moreno KO 6
Nov. 15 Tony Moreno Ricardo Delgado D 10

1974
Mar. 4 Terry Krueger Tom Berry KO 1
Mar. 11 Terry Krueger Otis Brown KO 1
Mar. 12 Terry Krueger Charlie Lee TKO 1
Sep. 17 Tony Moreno Manuel Rodriguez KO 4
Oct. 11 James Martinez Johnny Moreno W 10; Sergio Reyes Luis Rico KO 2

1976
Apr. 13 Mike Ayala Javier Moncivais W 10
Jun. 22 Mike Ayala Tony Rocha W 10
Jul. 27 Mike Ayala Goyo Vargas KO 4
Oct. 12 Jimmy Heair Rocky Ramon W 10
Oct. 26 Mike Ayala Ramon Elorde W 10
Nov. 17 Aug.in Estrada Maurice Watkins W 10

1977
Jan. 18 Mike Ayala Cesar Deciga KO 7
Feb. 8 Tony Moreno Candy Iglesias W 10

Mar. 25 Mike Ayala Romeo Anaya KO 6; Raul Ramirez Johnny Moreno KO 3
Mar. 26 Leroy Jones Dino Dennis W 8
Mar. 27 David Love Bobby Watts KO 4; Vonzell Johnson Tony Greene KO 4; Floyd Mayweather Miguel Barreto W 8; Greg Coverson Jerry Kornele W 8; James Martinez Warren Matthews W 8
Apr. 2 Ruben Castillo Walter Seeley W 10; Randall "Tex" Cobb Trinidad Escamilla KO 1; Saoul Mamby Mike Everett W 10
May 17 Rodolfo Martinez Mike Ayala KO 7
May 31 Rafael "Bazooka" Limon Aug.in Estrada W 10
Jun. 28 Alejo Rodriguez Norberto Rodriguez KO 1
Aug. 9 Mike Ayala Reynaldo Hidalgo W 10; Rodolfo Martinez Gilberto Illueca W 10; Sammy Ayala Edwardo Vega KO 1
Oct. 4 Mike Ayala Raul Tirado W 10
Nov. 8 Lupe Pintor Baby Kid Chocolate KO 2
Dec. 6 Ruben Olivares Ricky Gutierrez W 10; Mike Ayala Tarcisio Gomez W 10

1978
Jan. 30 Lupe Pintor Davey Vasquez KO 2; Sammy Ayala Victor Villanueva KO 7
Feb. 20 Carlos Mendoza Roy Hernandez KO 6; Rafael Duran Calvin Sheppard W 6; Gerardo Aceves Robert Vasquez KO 9
Mar. 18 Mike Ayala Ronnie McGarvey KO 1; Jorge Lujan Roberto Ruvaldino TKO 11; retains WBA bantamweight title, San Antonio's first World title fight.
Mar. 31 Alfredo Perez Juan Angel Villasana W 6
May 2 Adelaido Galindo Sergio Reyes W 10; Sammy Ayala Juan Ramirez KO 1
Jun. 20 Sammy Ayala Mike Everett KO 10
Jul. 18 Mike Ayala Edwin Alarcon W 10; Alejo Rodriguez Paulino Garcia KO 2
Aug. 22 Mike Ayala Shig Fukuyama KO 6
Sep. 19 Sammy Ayala Lupe Galindo KO 3
Nov. 21 Salvador Sanchez Edwin Alarcon TKO 9; Mike Ayala Edel Borunda W 12
Dec. 5 Sammy Ayala Jose Luis Baltazar W 10

1979
Jan. 30 Sammy Ayala Johnny Copeland W 10

Mar. 13 Salvador Sanchez James Martinez W 10
Jun. 17 Salvador Sanchez Fel Clemente W 12; Danny Lopez Mike Ayala KO 15, retains WBC Featherweight Title; Howard Davis Jose Hernandez KO 7; Sammy Ayala Johnny Copeland KO 7; Rocky Ramon Leonardo Bermudez W 10
Jul. 31 Roberto Reynosa Charlie Parker KO 1
Aug. 28 Fernando Montes Victor Rodriguez W 10; Danny Favella Leonardo Zapata KO 2; Sammy Ayala Rafael Nunez KO 3
Oct. 30 Rocky Ramon Angel Mata W 10
Nov. 3 Jim Watt Robert Vasquez KO 9 in Glasgow,Scotland; retains WBC lightweight title

1980
Mar. 22 Willie Rodriguez Rocky Ramon W 12 in Bethlehem, PA, USBA lLight welterweight title.
May 20 Felix Castillo Jose Salas KO 4
May 23 Mike Ayala Nicky Perez W 12 in Pontiac,MI; wins NABF super bantamweight title.
Jun. 17 Tony Ayala Zip Castillo KO 1; Sammy Ayala Norberto Rodriguez KO 2
Jul. 15 Tony Ayala German Marquez KO 1; Abel Herrera Rodolfo Guevarra W 6
Sep. 13 Salvador Sanchez Patrick Ford W 15, retains WBC featherweight title; Jaime Garza Calvin Sheppard KO 4; Alberto Davila Terry Pizzarro KO 6; Juan LaPorte Mano Morua W 10; Gaby Canizales Oscar Gomez K 6; Oscar Muniz Miguel Flores KO 3
Nov. 7 Tony Tubbs Ron Draper W 6; Lynn Ball Jody Ballard W 10; Mike Ayala Javier Flores W 10; Candido Tellez Candelario Iglesias KO 5
Ken Norton Randall "Tex" Cobb W 10

1981
Jan. 15 Johnny Bumphus Jose Angel Medina KO 2
Jan. 16 Donald Curry Juan Ramirez TKO 2; Tony Tucker Victor Rodriguez TKO 2; Tony Ayala Jose Luis Baltazar TKO 2; Alex Ramos Jose Pacheco KO 5
Feb. 10 Ray Boyd Sergio Salcedo KO 2
May 25 Randall "Tex" Cobb Harry Terrell KO 5

May 26 Tony Perea Vernon Johnston W
8; Louis Burke Gilbert Garza KO 3
May 27 Mike Ayala Sergio Castro W 10
Jul. 9 John Baca Leon Shaw KO 9;
Louis Burke Abel Herrera KO 3
Aug. 4 Mike Ayala Angel Lira KO 8
Aug. 23 Tony Ayala Nicanor Camacho W
10; Johnny Bumphus Dale Hernandez
KO 5; Mike Ayala Jose Resendez W 10
Aug. 30 Chris McDonald Lou Benson D 8
Nov. 3 Aaron Lopez Ed Bonilla KO 3

1982
Feb. 26 Tony Ayala Nat King KO 3;
Steve Cruz Juan Carlos Barbosa TKO
1; Sammy Ayala Sergio Aguirre KO 4
May 16 Gaby Canizales Ricardo Varela W 10
Jun. 23 Gaby Canizales Diego Rosario KO 5
Aug. 1 Tony Ayala Robbie Epps TKO 1;
Gaby Canizales Jose Torres W 10;
James Pipps Angel Lira KO 8; Aaron
Lopez Adolfo Marquez KO 1
Aug. 10 Steve Cruz Javier Barajas W 8
Oct. 20 Aaron Lopez Antonio Leal W 8;
Sammy Ayala Roberto Flores KO 3
Dec. 1 Aaron Lopez Jose Salas KO 6

1983
Feb. 26 Alexis Arguello Vilomar Fernandez
W 10; Kenny Baysmore Roland Avila KO
4; Marcos Villasana Gerald Hayes SD 10
Apr. 29 Mike Ayala Kenny Mitchell W 12;
retains NABF super bantamweight title.
Nov. 30 Mike Ayala Alejandro Garcia KO 2

1984
Mar. 21 Aaron Lopez Nicky Perez KO 8
Mar. 22 Mike Ayala Rodolfo Quinteros TKO 2
Jun. 6 Gaby Canizales Javier Diaz KO 2;
Mike Ayala Jesus Lopez TKO 4
Nov. 9 Orlando Canizales Reymundo Euresti
KO 1; Mike Ayala Rodolfo Martinez KO 6

1985
Feb. 6 Michael Arms Aldo Montes KO 6
Apr. 19 Juan Meza Mike Ayala KO 6 in
Inglewood,CA, retains WBC super
bantamweight title.
Sep. 10 Mike Ayala Pascual Aranda W 12
Dec. 13 Jesse Benavides Juan Armienta
KO 1

1986
Feb. 4 Gene Hatcher Kevin Austin W 10
Mar. 2 Mike Ayala Julian Solis W 10
Mar. 5 Grover Robinson Freddie Guzman
W 10
Apr. 15 Cassius Clay Horne Hector
Rodriguez KO 1
May 6 Orlando Canizales Javier Diaz W
10; Roque Montoya John Dobbins W
10 Jun. 5 Gilberto Contreras Lee Cargle W 8
Jul. 1 Robin Blake Juan Carlos Alvarado
KO 7; Edwin Rangel Richard Abila TKO
6; Ramiro Adames Rico Velasquez KO 1
Jul. 25 John Michael Johnson Jesse Alviar
W 4; Matthew Brooks Higinio Soreno
TKO 1; Mike Ayala Aaron Lopez W 12
Sep. 10 John Vasquez John Michael Johnson
W 4; Johnny Casas Ricky Avila W 4
Nov. 14 David Gonzalez Gustavo
Martinez KO 3
Dec. 6 Daniel Zaragoza Mike Ayala KO
7; Paulie Ayala Hector Cortez D 10

1987
Jan. 30 Orlando Canizales Prudencio
Cardona TKO 6; Gaby Canizales
Mauro Diaz W 10
Feb. 27 Alfred Rangel James Manning W 10
Mar. 15 John Michael Johnson Fernando
Puente KO 2; David Gonzalez Jerry
Venzor KO 5
Apr. 3 Daniel Zaragoza Aaron Lopez W
12; Johnny Casas Raul Sanchez TKO 2
Apr. 14 Martin Ortegon Randy Reedy W
6; Carlos Flores Jeff Hanna W 10
May 5 John Michael Johnson Anthony
Lopez TKO 2; Gaby Canizales Julio
Blanco W 10; Sylvester Kennon
Guadalupe Galvan TKO 4; Johnny Casas
Ramon Sosa TKO 3; Mike Ayala Raul
Lopez KO 2; Ray Medel Richard Abila W
10; Lonnie Beasley Carman Garcia KO 3
Jun. 19 Mike Ayala Arturo Tebaqui TKO 5
Aug. 15 Louie Espinoza Mike Ayala KO 9,
retains WBA junior featherweight title;
John Michael Johnson Jesse Alviar TKO
3; Jesse Benavides Arturo Tebaqui KO 3
Sep. 25 Orlando Canizales Jose Olivares
KO 4; JR Fraser Raymond Flores W 4
Nov. 10 John Michael Johnson John Vasquez
TKO 1; Raul Sanchez Raymond Flores D 4

Dec. 20 Ladislao Mijangos Leon Spinks W 10; Alfredo Ortiz Floyd Weaver D 4; Roland Rangel Alfred Ortiz D 4; Oscar Pena Lonnie Beasley KO 3

1988

Jun. 17 Ralph Reyes Anthony Chavez KO 1; JR Fraser Raymond Flores W 4; Ramon Medel Paul Gonzales W 12; Roland Rangel Alberto Santana W 4

Oct. 2 "Jesse" James Leija Oscar Davis TKO 1; Fidel Bassa Raymond Medel W 12, retains WBA flyweight title; Jesse Benavides Richard Abila W 10; Roland Rangel Raymond Flores W 4

Nov. 3 "Jesse" James Leija Martin Melendez TKO 2; Roland Rangel Alfonso Chavez TKO 1

Nov. 29 Orlando Canizales Jim Navarro KO 1; Steve Martinez Alfred Ortiz TKO 1; Harold Rhodes Ralph Reyes TKO 2; Roland Rangel JR Fraser W 6

1989

May 19 Angel Adame Oscar Davis TKO 1; Steve Martinez Jose Valero KO 1; Roland Rangel Jerry Perez W 6

Jul. 7 James Coker Wayne Corbett W 4; Angel Adame Javier Cruz W 4; Robert Quiroga Joey Olivo W 10

Oct. 17 Johnny Tapia John Michael Johnson W 8 in Phoenix,AZ

Dec. 1 James Coker Ron Nickles KO 1; Richard Salazar Angel Adame D 4; Roland Rangel Pat Barnes TKO 3

1990

Apr. 7 Joey Corpus Eugene Myles TKO 1

Apr. 21 Robert Quiroga Juan Polo Perez W 12 in Sunderland, England; Quiroga wins IBF junior bantamweight title

May 6 John Michael Johnson Rodolfo Robles KO 3; Alfred Rangel Tony Duran TKO 3; Roland Rangel Jose Luis Sanchez TKO 6; Edwin Rangel Carlos Ramirez TKO 5

Jun. 7 Jesus Salud Martin Ortegon TKO 11 in Honolulu,HI, wins vacant IBC super bantamweight title.

Aug. 14 Orlando Canizales Eddie Rangel KO 5 in Saratoga Springs, NY. retains

IBF bantamweight title

Sep. 25 Steve Cruz Benito Rodriguez W 10; Richard Salazar Alfonso Mallen TKO 2; Ruben Nevarez Tomas Barrientes W 4

Oct. 8 Edward Parker "Jesse" James Leija D 10; James Coker Miguel Barcenas KO 4

Nov. 18 Mike Ayala Victor Navarro KO 5

1991

Jan. 7 "Jesse" James Leija Felipe Dejesus W 10; Alex Rios Miguel Barcenas KO 1; Richard Salazar Noel Orozco W 6

Mar. 1 Martin Ortegon Alfonso Estrada KO 4 in Duluth, MN, wins IBC junior featherweight title

Mar. 2 John Michael Johnson Armando Diaz W 1; Angel Adame Raul Hernandez TKO 2

Apr. 12 Emmett Linton Richard Terrazas KO 3; Mike Ayala Lee Cargle W 1; Ruben Nevarez Conrad Sanchez TKO 4

Apr. 27 Alejandro Sanabria Edwin Rangel W 10; Angel Adame Noel Orozco W 6; Roland Rangel Pedro Rodriguez TKO 2

May 31 "Jesse" James Leija Miguel Arrozal DQ 8; Alex Rios Kevin Jones TKO 1; Oscar Pena Randy Cross TKO 2

Jun. 3 Troy Dorsey Alfred Rangel KO 1 in Las Vegas, wins vacant IBF featherweight title

Jun. 15 Thomas Tate Enrique Noriega TKO 4; Welcome Ncita Hurley Snead W 12; Robert Quiroga Akeem Anifowoshe W 12, retains IBF junior bantamweight title; Steve Martinez Jerry Grant W 8; Roland Rangel Alejandro Quiroz TKO 2

Aug. 16 John Michael Johnson Roland Gomez TKO 3; Edwin Rangel Jeff Whaley KO 1; Steve Martinez Jerry Grant W 8; Roland Rangel James Sudberry TKO 3

Dec. 11 Martin Ortegon Pedro Davila KO 4 in Duluth, MN, retains IBC junior featherweight title

1992

Jan. 20 Wayne Powell Oscar Pena SD 12

Mar. 3 "Jesse" James Leija Jose Luis Martinez TD 9; Tim Littles Antoine Byrd

W 12; Louie Leija Salvador Carrillo TKO 1; Alex Rios Armando Torres KO 1; Everardo Lerma Roland Rangel TKO 2

May 24 John Michael Johnson Abner Barajas W 12, USBA junior bantamweight title; Alex Rios Jose Lopez KO 2; Roland Rangel Natividad Chayrez TKO 3; Edwin Rangel Javier Diaz MD 8

Jul. 15 "Jesse" James Leija Jesus Poll W 10; Shane Blake Undra Hawkins TKO 2; Louie Leija Ivory Courtney TKO 2; Juan Martinez Benito Rodriguez W 6

Oct. 3 Raul Marquez Rafael Rezzaq TKO 4; "Jesse" James Leija Troy Dorsey TKO 6; Louie Leija Noel Orozco W 4; Alex Rios Jose Garcia W 4

Nov. 6 Raymond Flores Armando Torres KO 2; Alex Rios James Mason KO 3; Salvador Sanchez Aureo Dominguez W 6

Dec. 3 "Jesse" James Leija Gabriel Castro W 10

1993

Jan. 16 Adolpho Washington Drake Thadzi W 10; Philip Holiday Verdell Smith TKO 8; Ron Johnson Francois Nkuadi TKO 2; Julio Cesar Borboa Robert Quiroga TKO 12, wins IBF junior bantamweight title; Joseph Chingangu Tim Martin TKO 1

Feb. 12 Derrick James James Mason W 8

Feb. 25 Shane Blake Ron Martin W 4; Louie Leija Jacob Godinez TKO 2; Edward Escobedo Earl Talley KO 2; Jaime Lerma Roland Rangel W 8; Rodrigo Cerda Isaac Gomez SD 6

Mar. 23 David Tua Alfredo Nevarez TKO 1; Eddie Hopson Hector J. Monjardin TKO 6; Raul Marquez Jose Garcia KO 4; "Jesse" James Leija Louie Espinoza W 12, wins NABF featherweight title; Narciso Aleman Tony McCall W 4; Shane Blake Vastine Hill TKO 1; Louie Leija Vicente Castillo TKO 1

Apr. 21 Rodrigo Cerda Richard Robinson TKO 5

May 19 Ron Johnson Pedro Trevino TKO 1; Shane Blake Andrew Banks TKO 1; Eliseo Vela Juan Cortez W 4; Roland Rangel Griffin Coleman W 10

Jun. 21 John Michael Johnson Arturo Estrada TKO 6; Raymond Flores Albert Lopez TKO

1; Alex Rios Jose Garcia TKO 5

Jul. 19 Jesse Benavides Ramiro Valero KO 1; Calvin Lampkin Clinton Whitehead TKO 1; Louie Leija Manuel Robles TKO 3; Juan Martinez Raymond Flores D 6; Gerardo Velasquez Peter Ramirez TKO 2

Aug. 26 John Michael Johnson Rodolfo Robles TKO 6; Gene Hatcher Simon Moya KO 4; Juan Martinez Richard Salazar W 10

Sep. 3 Golden Johnson Chris George TKO 1; Louie Leija Joaquin Escobar TKO 2

Sep. 10 Frank Tate Everardo Armenta TKO 9; Robin Reid Jose Garcia W 6; Terron Millett Ruben Gonzales W 4; Terry Norris Joe Gatti KO 1, retains WBC light middleweight title; Thomas Tate Eduardo Ayala W 10; Tim Austin Hector Lara TKO 1; "Jesse" James Leija Azumah Nelson D 12, for the WBC super featherweight title; Julio Cesar Chavez Pernell Whitaker D 12, for the WBC welterweight title; Levander Johnson Bobby Brewer TKO 10; Ernesto Magdaleno Tim Bryan TKO 2

Oct. 13 Ron Johnson Simon Moya TKO 3; Paulie Ayala Arturo Estrada W 6; Yakini McKinney Anthony Mandujano TKO 1

Nov. 23 Alex Rios Ramon Felix TKO 2; Raymond Flores Richard Salazar W 10

Dec. 7 Jesse Benavides Jesus Sarabia W 12

Dec. 8 Louie Leija Angel Fernandez TKO 1

Dec. 22 John Michael Johnson Arturo Estrada TKO 8; Gilbert Salinas Manuel Sepeda D 4

1994

Feb. 17 Golden Johnson Jaime Herrera TKO 2

Mar. 3 "Jesse" James Leija Tomas Valdez KO 3

Mar. 23 Jaime Lerma Ahmed Alaajiy TD 3; Charles Daughtry Shane Blake TKO 2; Louie Leija Eduardo Montes TKO 6; Edward Escobedo Doug Norris TKO 1; Sergio Reyes Javier Diaz W 10

Apr. 22 John Michael Johnson Junior Jones KO 11 in Las Vegas, wins WBA bantamweight title

May 7 "Jesse" James Leija Azumah Nelson W 12 in Las Vegas, wins WBC super featherweight title

Jul. 16 Daorung Chuvatana John Michael
Johnson TKO 1 in Uttaradit,Thailand,
wins WBA bantamweight title
Aug. 19 Jesus Chavez Rudy Hernandez
W 4; Louie Leija Eduardo Castillo TKO
1; Jamie Lerma Robert Lane TKO 2;
Yakini McKinney Porfirio Mendoza TKO
1; Eldon Sneed Manuel Mendez TKO 1
Sep. 17 Gabriel Ruelas "Jesse" James
Leija W 12 in Las Vegas, wins WBC
super featherweight title
Nov. 19 Louie Espinoza Julian Flores
KO 7; Louie Leija Jose Garcia TKO 3

1995
Jan. 7 Alejandro Gonzalez Kevin Kelley
TKO 10; Wilfredo Vasquez Orlando
Canizales SD 12; Carlos Gerena Jesus
Chavez SD 8; Ancee Gedeon Robert
Quiroga W 8; Darryl Pinckney Louie Leija
KO 1; Carlos Monroe Sean Rickards
TKO 2; Danny Rios Luis Fernando
Acosta W 4; Dezi Ford Dan Reyes W 6
Jan. 31 Ed Tobar Emanuel Aug.us W 8
Tomas Barrientes Manuel Sepeda W 8
May 24 David Donnis Danny Cordova W
4; Mike Trejo Orlando Rodriguez TKO
3; Tomas Barrientes Sam Miller W 10
May 27 Gilbert Salinas Golden Johnson D
4; Harold Warren Hector Ulises Chong W
10; Ericel Nucamendi Louie Leija W 8;
Rudy Hernandez Emmanuel Ford W 6
Jul. 19 Danny Rios Golden Johnson D 6;
Mike Trejo Francisco Cruz KO 1; Anthony
Townsend Tate Gonzales D 4; Alex Rios
Jerry Stephens TKO 3; Frankie Gonzalez
Alphonso Reyes TKO 2
Jul. 29 Alex Sanchez Tomas Rivera W 12;
Danny Romero Miguel Martinez KO 6;
Roberto Garcia Francisco Segura TKO 1;
"Jesse" James Leija Rodney Garnett KO
7; Cesar Soto Jose Luis Madrid TKO 6;
Jesus Chavez Arturo Rangel KO 2; Juan
Carlos Rodriguez Mauro Lucero D 12
Sep. 14 Lupe Miranda Emanuel Aug.us W
8; Steve Trumble Angel Fernandez
TKO 2; Mike Trejo Juan Cortez TKO 2;
Richard Armstrong Abel Davila TKO 3
Dec. 15 Oscar De La Hoya "Jesse"
James Leija TKO 2 in New York City,
retains WBO lightweight title

1996
Jan. 24 John Michael Johnson Lazaro
Padilla W 8; Danny Rios Jerry Cooper
TKO 6; Victor Urbina Danny Rios W
8; Francois Nkuadi Angel Adame D 6
Apr. 30 Johnny Tapia Ramon Gonzalez
KO 2; Rafael Ruelas Tomas Barrientes
KO 2; Eric "Butterbean" Esch Richard
Davis KO 1; Arturo Ramos Rodrigo
Garcia KO 1; Louie Leija Roberto Avila
W 8; Jabbar Hurd Mike Trejo D 4
Jun. 1 Azumah Nelson "Jesse" James
Leija TKO 6 in Las Vegas, retains
WBC super featherweight title
Sep. 10 Mike Trejo Jesus Cuervito Garcia
KO 2; Danny Rios Jorge Loya TKO 3;
James Coker David Williams W 6; Victor
Rodriguez Reynaldo Ramirez KO 2

1997
Mar. 3 Jesus Chavez Louie Leija TKO 6
in Austin, wins Vacant NABF
superflyweight title
Mar. 8 James Coker Charles Scott TKO
5; Danny Rios Julian Romero W 8;
Vince Marbley Efrain Garcia KO 5;
Joe Morales Fernando Ibarra W 4;
Victor Rodriguez Juan Segovia TKO 3
Mar. 22 "Jesse" James Leija Joel Perez
W 12 in Corpus Christi, wins vacant
NABF lightweight title
Apr. 19 Melchor Castro Miguel Martinez
TKO 11; John Michael Johnson Jesus
Montiel TKO 4; Mike Trejo Pedro Sanchez
W 6; Adrian Reyes Alejandro Orta TKO 2
May 8 James Coker James Scott TKO 8
in Dallas, wins WBC Continental
Americas junior middleweight title
Jun. 14 Floyd Mayweather Larry O'Shields
W 6; Genaro Hernandez Anatoly
Alexandrov SD 12; "Jesse" James Leija
Jose Rodriguez W 8; Arturo Ramos Raul
Zavala KO 1; Eric Morel Armando Diaz W
4; Mikhail Krivolapov Guadalupe Rodriguez
KO 3; Oscar De La Hoya David Kamau KO
2, retains WBC welterweight title
Aug. 9 Carlos Alberto Martinez Victor
Rodriguez W 4
Aug. 30 Adrian Reyes Antonio Martinez W 4
Sep. 10 Harold Warren Jose Luis Montes
KO 1; John Michael Johnson Martin

Solorio TKO 5; Mike Trejo Juan Velasquez KO 2; Armando Guerrero Juan Delgado W 4; Adrian Reyes Rafael Arroyo W 4

Nov. 22 Jesse Gutierrez Jose Guadalupe Favila TKO 1; Mike Trejo Ruben Contreras TKO 1; Adrian Reyes Antonio Garcia TKO 3; Jay Cantu Jose Ibarra TKO 2

1998

Jan. 20 Diosbelys Hurtado Aaron Zarate KO 1; "Jesse" James Leija Joel Perez W 12, retains NABF lightweight title; Golden Johnson Cesar Delgado W 6; Arturo Ramos Jose Guadalupe Favila TKO 2; Lovey Page Thurman Blanton KO 3; Louie Leija Guadalupe Rodriguez KO 2

Mar. 27 James Coker Jose Cataneo KO 6; Joe Morales Juan Delgado W 4; Gilbert Salinas Antonio Garcia W 6; Rodrigo Cerda Oscar Garcia W 6

May 1 James Coker Buck Smith KO 8; Adan Vargas Ancee Gedeon W 12; Gregorio Vargas Cesar Delgado KO 2; "Jesse" James Leija Troy Crain KO 2; Lance Whitaker Ray Butler TKO 6; Arturo Ramos Antonio Garcia KO 1; Carlos Alberto Martinez German Castro W 8

Jul. 7 Ben Tackie Louie Leija TKO 8, retains IBA Americas lightweight title; Lovey Page Ray Butler KO 1; Danny Perez Anthony Townsend TKO 2; James Coker Robert West W 12; Rodrigo Cerda Ricardo Barrera W 8; Rudy Martinez Roman Trejo W 4; Carlos Alberto Martinez Rudy Hernandez TKO 4

Jul. 11 Gabriel Ruelas Troy Dorsey TKO 6; Gregorio Vargas Tracy H. Patterson TKO 6; Miguel Angel Gonzalez Alexis Perez TKO 5; "Jesse" James Leija Azumah Nelson W 12; Hector Camacho Troy Crain W 6; Arturo Ramos Joel Garcia W 6; Michael Lerma Noe Fuentes TKO 1

Aug. 5 John Michael Johnson Arturo Estrada W 8; Roland Rangel Booker Kidd TKO 2; Joe Morales Jose Montoya KO 5; Hector Chavez Kleimer Hernandez TKO 1; Joey Flores James Perez TKO 4; Chris Martinez Jeff Clayton TKO 3

Aug. 25 Jesse Gutierrez Emmanuel Ford KO 1; Sep. 10 Cliff Nellon Lewis Gilbert

KO 1; Andres Esquivel Miguel Gonzalez W 4; Danny Flores Natalio Ponce W 4; Chris Martinez Joey Flores D 4; Mariano Gonzalez Kleimer Hernandez TKO 1

Nov. 14 Shane Mosley "Jesse" James Leija TKO 9 in Mashantucket, CT, retains IBF lightweight title

Nov. 17 Lovey Page Wesley Martin TKO 1; Danny Rios David Armstrong W 8; Rudy Hernandez Roland Rangel W 8; Mack Mclin David Donnis W 8; Mike Trejo Mariano Gonzalez W 12

1999

May 29 Lehlo Ledwaba John Michael Johnson W 12 Johannesburg, South Africa , wins vacant IBF junior featherweight title

Jun. 4 Lemuel Nelson Louie Leija TKO 5 in Biloxi, MS, wins vacant WBA North American lightweight title

Aug. 20 "Jesse" James Leija Verdell Smith W 10; Tony Ayala Manuel Esparza TKO 3; James Coker Eduardo Gutierrez TKO 8; Harold Warren Troy Crain W 8; Tim Scoggins Jarred Kemp KO 1; Omar Davila Rafael Ramirez W 4; Roberto Elizondo Juan Segovia W 4; Manuel Rodriguez Chris Medina W 4

Sep. 9 Arturo Ramos John Frazier W 4; Carlos Ramirez Miguel Angel Olivares TKO 7; Omar Davila Andres Esquivel TKO 1; Alex Rios Jose Cataneo TKO 4; Danny Flores Joel Tienda TD 4

Nov. 6 Mike Trejo Eduardo Manzano KO 4; Alex Rios Lionel Ortiz D 8; Carlos Ramirez Jesse Gutierrez KO 1; Danny Flores Natalio Ponce W 6; Joey Flores Ruben Coronado TKO 1; Omar Davila Juan Carlos Herrera MD 4

Dec. 11 Carlos Contreras Carlos Navarro W 12; Tony Ayala Tony Menefee TKO 4; James Coker Urbano Gurrola W 10; Jose Luis Baltazar Arturo Ramos D 6; Joe Morales Luis Perez W 6; Orlando Hollis Rudy Hernandez W 8

2000

Mar. 16 Omar Davila Juan Manuel Herrera SD 6; Joe Morales Juan Carlos Martinez W 8; Jesse Gutierrez Larry O'Shields W 6; Danny Flores Juan Velasquez W 4;

Juan Carlos Herrera Jaime Morales ; MD 4; Roberto Lopez Enrique Jupiter W 12

Apr. 14 Tony Ayala Jorge Luis Vado KO 4; "Jesse" James Leija Jorge Luis Lopez KO 3; Edward Escobedo Wesley Martin TKO 2; Jesse Gonzalez Mathias Bedburdick W 6; James Coker Shane Blake TKO 4

Jun. 11 Jesse Gutierrez Juan Carlos Aranday TKO 5; Jaime Morales Omar Davila SD 6; Gabriel Elizondo Arturo Velasquez TKO 2; Jose Angel Macias Jerome Lockett W 4; John Gonzalez Carlos De La Cruz TKO 3

Jul. 8 Efren Hinojosa Steve Quinonez SD 12; Nick Acevedo Richard Lee Hall TKO 3; Jesse Gonzalez Roland Rangel TKO 3; Jesse Gutierrez Jose Narvaez TKO 6; Richard Best Jerome Lockett TKO 2

Jul. 28 Yory Boy Campas Tony Ayala TKO 9; Tito Mendoza James Coker MD 10; Andres Esquivel Raymond Gomez W 4; Leonel Herrera Jaime Morales SD 6; Gabriel Elizondo Richard Pasillas W 4; Quinton Whitaker Shane Stephens TKO 3; Rogelio Barron Juan Campeon MD 4

Sep. 16 Jaime Morales Angel Adame MD 8; Oct. 29 Gabriel Elizondo Roman Trejo TKO 5; Quinton Whitaker Jose Angel Macias KO 1; Raymond Gomez Sergio Reyes Jr SD 4; Erik Rodriguez Gabriel Hernandez KO 1

Nov. 2 Mike Trejo Hugo Romero TD 11; Danny Flores Jacobo Gomez W 6; James Elizalde Jesus Valadez W 4; Luke Leal Joey Flores W 6; Ron Simms Tremayne Hines TKO 2; Luis Hernandez Robert Martinez TKO 1

2001

Jan. 21 Jesse Gutierrez Rolando Reyes MD 8; Santiago Samaniego Jason Papillion W 10; Justin Juuko Antonio Ramirez TKO 9; Gabriel Elizondo James Harris II TKO 3; Omar Davila Charles Sims TKO 1; Abdias Castillo Raymond Gomez W 4

Feb. 10 Adan Vargas Jorge Eliecer Julio W 12; Joe Morales Jose Ayala W 8; Jesse Gutierrez Emmanuel Ford TKO 1; Erik Rodriguez Tomas Villa TKO 4; Omar Davila Starr Johnson KO 1; Alex Rios Shannon Miller W 6

Mar. 16 Oscar Diaz Johnny Joe Ramos

TKO 2; Manuel Sepeda Danny Flores D 6; Danny Rios Jamie Morales W 8; Nelson Alexander Angel Adame W 6; Jose Angel Macias Stacy Guzman TKO 2; Erik Rodriguez Chris Ortiz W 4; Robert Martinez Luis Torres TKO 2

Mar. 22 Omar Gonzalez Jorge Saucedo SD 4; Golden Johnson Bobby Heath TKO 6; Gabriel Elizondo Alejandro Moreno TKO 6; Joe Morales Jorge Reyes TKO 2; Omar Davila Jorge Luis Lopez KO 6; Ron Simms Sebastian Hill TKO 1; Eloy Suarez Robert Tapia TKO 1

Apr. 26 James Coker Kassim Ouma Tech D 2 in Dallas, for WBC Continental Americas junior middleweight title

Jun. 1 Kelvin Davis Bobby Scoggins TKO 2; Oscar Diaz Richard Best KO 1; Gabriel Elizondo Eliseo Vela W 6; Omar Davila Omar Duarte TKO 6; Jesse Gutierrez Jesse Lara SD 8; TJ Wilson Frederick Gatica W 4; Troy Ross Tim Scoggins TKO 1

Jun. 17 Calvin Brock Shawn Woods TKO 1; Kevin Petty Adam Richards TKO 3; Oscar Diaz Gonzalo Bonilla TKO 1; Eloy Suarez Raymond Gomez w 4; Joe Morales Carlos Contreras TKO 11, wins vacant NABA featherweight title; Gabriel Elizondo Roberto Gomez TKO 3; Erik Rodriguez Jesse Ruiz W 4

Jul. 31 Carmelo Ramos Cardyl Finley W 4; Ron Simms Marcus Harvey KO 1; Hicklet Lau Danny Rios W 10; Gabriel Elizondo Leonardo Gutierrez W 4; Tony Ayala Santos Cardona W 10; Steve Martinez Joe Rodriguez TD 2

Aug. 25 Oscar Diaz Jonathan Nelson TKO 2; Erik Rodriguez Mike Dobbs TKO 1; Dante Craig Dyirell Crayton TKO 4; Curtis Meeks Amado Arreola TKO 1; James Kirkland Maurice Chalmers TKO 3; Omar Davila Jaime Morales W 8; Ruben Garza Mack McLin W 4

Sep. 23 Gabriel Elizondo Glenn Donaire W 6; John Michael Johnson Harold Grey KO 7; Jose Rodriguez Mark Favella TKO 2; Joel Salas Ronnie Johnson TKO 1; Ron Simms Rosario Castillo KO 1

Nov. 1 Danny Flores Oscar Martinez W 4; Luis Muriel Leo Cardenas KO 1; Wayne Boudreaux Danny Rios TD 2; Carlos

Ramirez Jose Luis Noyola SD 8; Jorge Garcia Brandon Jackson TKO 2; Tomas Villa Jose Rodriguez TD 2; Jonathan Nelson Michael Soberanis TKO 3

Nov. 2 Oscar Diaz Felson Perez TKO 2; Carlos Diaz Erik Rodriguez D 8; Robert Guerrero Oscar Rosales W 4; Mauricio Pastrana Alberto Ontiveros TKO 9; Maurice Chalmers Joe Rodriguez KO 1

Nov. 9 Tony Ayala Manuel Lopez TKO 2; Paolo Vidoz Nick Nurse W 6; Gabriel Elizondo Raul Puga KO 2; Irene Pacheco Mike Trejo TKO 4; Omar Davila Dan Reyes W 6; Miguel Espino Maurice Chalmers W 4; Quinton Whitaker Ruben Navarro MD 4; Dominick Guinn Todd Diggs KO 1

2002

Jan. 5 Ricardo Williams Mark Adams TKO 4; Brian Viloria Antonio Perez TKO 3; Jose Navarro Eliseo Vela TKO 4; Jerson Ravelo Eric Olds TKO 1; Leonard Dorin Raul Horacio Balbi SD 12; Tito Mendoza Bruce Rumbolz TKO 3; Rocky Juarez Frank Martinez TKO 4; Danny Flores Juan Carlos Martinez W 8; "Jesse" James Leija Mickey Ward TD 5

Jan. 13 Oscar Diaz Jaime Morales W 8; Omar Davila Amado Navarro W 8; Adrian Reyes Charles Sims W 4; Curtis Meeks Randy Alonso W 4; Julio Quintanilla Jesus Camacho W 4; Brian Soto Jorge Garcia W 4

Jan. 25 Ron Simms Carlos Bunema W 6; Jorge Saucedo Charlie Estrada W 4; Ernest Reyes Anthony Flores KO 2; Brian Romero Juan De Los Santos KO 1; Jonathan Nelson Joey Flores TKO 3

Feb. 16 Joan Guzman Armando Guerrero W 10; Kermit Cintron Omar Davila TKO 2; Edson Madrid Anderson Santos W 6

Apr. 19 Omar Davila Awel Abdulai W 6; Gilbert Salinas Alex Reyes SD 4; Curtis Meeks Juan Villanueva TKO 1; Ron Simms Mack Willis TKO 4; Brian Soto Ron McCoy W 4; Shaun George Isaac Broussard W 4

May 3 Gabriel Elizondo Manny Melchor TKO 7; Jose Nieves Fidencio Reyes TKO 1; Eloy Suarez Quinton Whitaker W 4; Tony Ayala Urbano Gurrola KO 2; Rocky Lopez James Hall TKO 1;

Yacob Abraham Jerron Lockett D 4

Jun. 21 James Coker Alex Rios W 8; Yacob Abraham Anthony Flores TKO 1; Jesus Rodriguez Carlos Escobedo D 4; Charles Spear Rocky Lopez TKO 2; Eloy Suarez Jesse Gonzalez MD 4

Jun. 28 Jesus Chavez Julio C. Sanchez-Leon TKO 7; Armando Guerrero Sal Garcia W 8; Oscar Diaz John Trigg W 6; Brock Groom Ilia Tcharikov W 4; Danny Flores Ronnie Longakit W 6; Juan Carlos Aranday Luis Alonzo W 4

Aug. 16 Joe Morales Carlos Diaz W 8; Charles Spear Undra Hawkins KO 2; Ron Simms Alberto Albaladejo TKO 1; Charlie Estrada Thomas Heaton TKO 3

Aug. 24 Omar Davila Michael Davis W 8; Erik Rodriguez Jerry Cooper TKO 1; Emmanuel Ford Alberto Rendon MD 6; Brian Soto Robert Beham TKO 1; Curtis Meeks Chris Regular W 4

Oct. 11 Juan Carlos Rubio Alejandro Jimenez SD 8; Oscar Diaz Omar Davila KO 5; Erik Rodriguez Alberto Cepeda TKO 2; Shaun George Johnny Walker TKO 1; James Kirkland Edgar Pedraza W 4; Alexis Mejias Abdullah Rahman MD 4; Curtis Meeks Wayne Fletcher W 4; Kendall Holt Kevin Carter TKO 1

Dec. 3 Ron Simms Darmel Castillo TKO 9; Richard Ueding Yacob Abraham MD 4; Nick Gonzalez Deric Flores W 4

2003

Jan. 31 Oscar Diaz Benito Rodriguez TKO 5; Eloy Suarez Victor Lares KO 3; T.J. Wilson Willie Lee Kemp UD 6; James Kirkland Juan Carlos Aranday KO 3; Troy Ross Sam Reese KO 3; Erik Kirkland Allen Smith TKO1

Apr. 5 Jesse Ortiz Gary Mims TKO 1; Ramon Gomez Roger Salinas TKO 1; Juan Martin Ramirez Yacob Abraham SD 4; Francisco Villa Deric Flores UD 4; Maurice Chalmers Daniel Whitaker UD 4

May 16 Erik Rodriguez Jason Adams UD 10; Joe Morales Antonio Cermeno UD 10; Oscar Diaz Jeremiah Torres TKO 2; Ramon Gomez Omar Davila TKO 2; Yacob Abraham Jesse Ortiz UD 4; Adrian Reyes Jacobo Gomez UD 6

May 22 "Jesse" James Leija Adan Casillas
TKO 4; Israel Vazquez Jorge Eliecer Julio
TKO 10; Americo Santos Jesus Rodriguez
TKO 5; Richard Odoms Victor Moore UD
4; Ramon Gomez Donald Jenkins UD 4
Aug. 21 Gilbert Salinas Jacobo Gomez
UD 8; Jesse Ortiz Juan Martin Ramirez

W 4; Dan Uranga Robert Tapia KO 3;
Anthony Lucio Tommy Ellis TKO 3
Aug. 30 Erik Rodriguez Natalio Ponce MD
8; Adrian Reyes Yacob Abraham UD 6;
Omar Davila Luis Alonso UD 6; Fidencio
Reyes Charlie Estrada TKO 3; Gustavo
Zamora Daniel Martinez TKO 1

Exhibitions

1882
John L. Sullivan

1905
John L. Sullivan vs. Jake Kilrain

1924
Jun. 3 Jack Dempsey vs Ray Newman,
Marty Cutler and Curtis "Tex" Meeks,
each 2 rounds

1925
Sep. Jack Dempsey vs. four partners

1931
Mar. 3 George Godfrey vs George
Dilworth,Frank Nelson and Son
Goodrich, each two rounds
Mar. 9 Max Schmeling, vs. Pedro Lopez
(2 rounds),Lou Barba (1 round)

1937
Mar. 26 Joe Louis vs Leonard Dixon (4),
Homer "Red" Wilson (1), Seal Harris
(2); Billy Deeg Pelon Lopez TKO 8;

Kid Johnson Press Kinsey TKO 2; KO
Borado Kid Louis W 6; George
Dilworth Gunboat Smith TKO 4

1944
Sep. 27 Fritzie Zivic vs. Billy Grombacher
and Joey Yarosz, each 2 rounds

1951
Jan. 31 World Heavyweight Champion
Charles vs Ezzard Charles Dave
Hamza, Ezzard Charles, Bob Dixon,
Bob Wright, Bob Washington, Don St
Romain, Jim Maririas, Jesse Bragg,
Carroll Humphreys

1959
Sep. 12 World Bantamweight Champion
Becerra vs. Jose Becerra, Jesse Leija,
4 rounds

1972
Oct. 24 Muhammad Ali vs. Elmo
Henderson (2 rounds), Ronnie Right
(23), Sonny Moore (3), Terry Daniels (3)

Bibliography

Brown, Gerry, and Michael Morrison. *2003 Information Please Sports Almanac*. New York: Hyperion, 2003.

Carroll, Bob, et al. *Total Football*. New York: HarperCollins, 1977.

Dodd, William. *The History of the Texas League of Professional Baseball Clubs 1888–1951*. New York: Mead & Co.

Filichia, Peter. *Professional Baseball Franchises*. New York: Facts on File, 1993.

Fleischer, Nat. *The Ring Record Book and Boxing Encyclopedia*. New York: Ring Book Shop, 1954.

Hoie, Bob, and Carlos Bauer. *The Historical Register: The Complete Major and Minor League Register of Baseball's Greatest Players*. San Diego: Baseball Press Books, 1998.

Hollander, Zander. *The American Encyclopedia of Soccer*. New York: Everest House, 1980.

_____. *The Complete Encyclopedia of Hockey*. Detroit: Gale Research, 1993.

Holmes, Jon. *Texas Sport*. Austin: Texas Monthly Press, 1984.

Holway, John. *Blackball Stars: Negro Leagues Pioneers*. Westport, CT: Meckler, 1988.

_____. *The Complete Book of Baseball's Negro Leagues*. Fern Park, FL: Hastings House, 2001.

_____. *Voices From the Great Black Baseball Leagues*. 1975.

Hubbard, Jan. *The Official NBA Basketball Encyclopedia*. New York: Doubleday, 2000.

James, Tom. *San Antonio Spurs Media Guides, 1994* and *2002*. San Antonio: San Antonio Spurs, 1994 and 2002.

Johnson, Lloyd. *The Minor League Register*. Durham: Baseball America, 1994.

_____ and Miles Wolff. *The Encyclopedia of Minor League Baseball*. Durham, NC: Baseball America, 1993.

Kayser, Tom, and Scott Hanzelka. *2002 Texas League Official Media Guide and Record Book*. San Antonio: Texas League, 2002.

Mendell, Ronald L. *Who's Who in Baseball*. New Rochelle, NY: Arlington House, 1973.

_____. *Who's Who in Basketball*. New Rochelle, NY: Arlington House, 1973.

Myers, K. Jaguar. *The 2003 Sports Marketplace Directory*. Scottsdzale, AZ: Sportsguide, 2003.

O'Neal, Bill. *The Texas League 1888–1987: A Century of Baseball*. Austin: Eakin Press, 1987.

Peterson, Robert. *Only the Ball Was White.* New York: Gramercy Books, 1970.

Recht, Mike. *Official ABA Guide, 1974–75.* St. Louis: The Sporting News, 1974.

Riley, James A. *The Biographical Encyclopedia of the Negro Baseball Leagues.* New York: Carrol & Graf, 1994.

Ruggles, William B. *Texas League Record Book 1888–1961.* San Antonio: Texas League, 1962.

Shatzkin, Mike. *The Ballplayers.* New York: William Morrow, 1990.

Tarango, Martin. *Basketball Biographies.* Jefferson, NC: McFarland, 191.

Thorn, John, and Pete Palmer and Michael Gershman. *Total Baseball.* Kingston, NY: Total Sports, 2001.

Witt, Wayne. *San AntonioSpurs Media Guide, 1986–87.* San Antonio: San Antonio Missions, 1986.

_____. *San Antonio Missions Media Guides, 1994* and *1995.* San Antonio: San Antonio Missions, 1994 and 1995.

Other Sources

Also useful were back issues of the *San Antonio Light*, *San Antonio Express-News* and the weekly *San Antonio Register*, which provided a wealth of information on African-American sports not readily available elsewhere. Game programs from the Spurs, Missions, Tejanos, Gunslingers, Riders, Force, Texans, Iguanas, Dragons and Rampage were a great help with biographical information on players and coaches.

Among those who helped through letters, e-mails, interviews on San Antonio sports history are Robert Bradley, Bobby Bragan, Harry Bright, Jim Burris, Dick Butler, Dan Cook, Lou Fitzgerald, Chuck Harrison, Sam Harshaney, Mickey Holt, Tom Kayser, Elmer Kosub, Don LeJohn, Jodie McCarley, Von McDaniel, Stan McIlvaine, Bob Ostrum, George Pasterchick, John Pavlick Jr., Leo Posada, Barry Robinson, Morris Steevens, Amanda Tate, John Trowbridge, Jerry Wilton and Wayne Witt.

Collections of files and stories were also made available by the San Antonio Main Library and by several individuals, some no longer living: Ward Burris, Scott Hanzelka, Bob Hoie, Jerry Jackson, Fred Mosebach, Ray Nemec, Dick Peebles, William B. Ruggles and Harold Scherwitz.

Website sources include:

arenafan.com
boxrec.com
cfl.ca
cyberboxingzone.com
eteamz.com/minorleaguehalloffame
geocities.com/Colosseum/1871
hockeydb.com
hometown.aol.com/bradleyrd/apbr.html
members.aol.com/Amerfoot/afa.htm
nba.com
nba.com/spurs
oursportscentral.com/usfl/gunslrs.htm
remembertheaba.com
remembertheusfl.8m.com/main.html
samissions.com
sarampage.com
semiprofootball.org/index.htm
sover.net/~spectrum
sportsillustrated.cnn.com
texas-league.com
usbasket.com
wflfootball.tripod.com

Index to Text